CULTURE and POVERTY

CULTURE and POVERTY

Critique and Counter-Proposals

Charles A. Valentine

THE UNIVERSITY OF CHICAGO PRESS

CHICAGO AND LONDON

ISBN: 0-226-84545-1 (clothbound); 0-226-84547-8 (paperbound)
Library of Congress Catalog Card Number: 68-16718
THE UNIVERSITY OF CHICAGO PRESS, CHICAGO 60637
The University of Chicago Press, Ltd., London

Printed in the United States of America

Affectionately and Respectfully Dedicated

To My Mother

And the Memory of My Father

Preface

This is an ambitious essay. It is ambitious because in it I have tried to go beyond what has already been said on those much-discussed subjects, the poor and their ways of life. Moreover, I have attempted the difficult task of writing both as a scholar and as a citizen, hoping to address not only academic or other specialists but fellow citizens as well. This attempt stems from my strong conviction that there must be many lines of mutual relevance between two spheres that are sometimes artificially separated. The first of these is the realm of fact-finding, systematic knowledge, and theory-building in the human sciences. The second is the sphere of social policy, political problems, and ideological issues. So the following pages contain considerable commentary on social problems and questions of value judgment related to poverty. I have tried to highlight some of the many interconnections of these concerns and the problems of gaining knowledge and understanding of the poor and their place in society. The basic subject matter treated here is the work of professional specialists in several of the human sciences. Particular attention is given to implications of this work for more general problems that affect everyone in society, directly or indirectly.

In addition to being ambitious, this effort is sometimes presumptuous, in the sense of being assertive beyond the bounds of modesty often observed in academic writing. Clearly, many specialists, including a number whose works are analyzed critically in the following chapters, have greater knowledge and experience of various matters discussed here than I. I have nevertheless presumed to comment, sometimes boldly, on both scientific and ideological issues raised in the works of these experts. Four convictions have prompted me to do this. First, I believe that practical political problems and ideological issues stemming from the continued existence of poverty in the contemporary world will drastically determine the immediate future of society. Second, I hope that scholarship and science can contribute to the constructive resolution of these problems, but I fear that so far the net effect of professional expertise in these fields has been predominantly pernicious. Third, I am convinced that these difficulties have received far too little attention and discussion, with the dangerous consequence that ill-founded conclusions and recommendations from the academic experts are being accepted and acted upon by the public and policy makers alike. Finally, with considerable hesitation and anxiety, I have reached the judgment that my own background and experience, despite substantial gaps and deficiencies, are sufficient so that I cannot evade the citizen's obligation to speak out.

The last point perhaps requires that the reader be given more than the usual minimum basis for making his own evaluation of the author's qualifications. By this I mean a basis apart from the conventional indications of formal professional status or the internal evidence of the pages which follow. I have had no extensive career of systematic firsthand research among the poor. Since childhood, my principal direct exposure to poverty in our own society has been through intensive participation in the civil rights movement in several American cities over a period of more than five years. While this movement, of course, has not often been predominantly populated by the poor, nevertheless this experience has been relevant. My experience in this context has involved systematic research, including some informal field work. Most of my formal knowledge of poverty in America, however, stems from reading and library research.

My ethnographic experience as an anthropologist was gained in a quite different, though not wholly irrelevant, context. On two expeditions to the Pacific island territory of New Guinea, I was able to study the effects of poverty and relative deprivation on native peoples in the highly stratified plural society of a colonial dependency. It should be clear, then, that my arguments for anthropological approaches to poverty studies in complex societies cannot be supported by what would perhaps be the ideal validation. That is, I cannot yet report results from an urban ethnographic study of my own among the poor. Hence the research suggestions made here necessarily have a somewhat prospective, programmatic quality. It may well be argued that the prospective research should have been carried out before I composed this essay. While there is merit in this argument, the urgency of the concerns and convictions expressed above ultimately persuaded me to disregard it.

Many people have been most helpful and generous with their time and knowledge in discussing the issues raised here. I have learned from each of them, even though I have not always accepted their suggestions for improvements. Among those who helped most in this way are John Atkins, Helen Gouldner, James and Rose Marie Jaquith, Joseph Kahl, Eleanor Leacock, Lee Rainwater, Kenneth Read, Harry and Irma Rosen, Steven Schwartzchild, Michael Seltzer, Edward and Joan Singler, Norman Whitten, and Alvin Wolfe. Peggy Stinson and Irene Brown patiently and efficiently supervised the preparation of drafts. I am indebted to the Department of Sociology-Anthropology, Washington University, for funds supporting this preparation. My most devoted discussant, effective editor, tireless typing aid, and ceaseless source of support, however, has always been my wife Betty Lou.

CHARLES A. VALENTINE

Contents

Contents

Contents

1   Introduction: Uses and Abuses of the Idea of Culture

ANTHROPOLOGY AND THE MEANING OF CULTURE

The concept of culture, as used in the parlance of the human sciences, arose from a great human confrontation. The idea of culture was one of the principal intellectual outgrowths of the worldwide meeting between the expansionist West and exotic non-Western peoples. The confrontation began with the contacts of exploration and matured into the relationships of empire. From this experience the West derived a growing need to find order in its increasing knowledge of immensely varied human lifeways. As the emerging science of anthropology developed the culture concept, it thereby provided an important means to this end of discovering order in variation.

Three aspects of the culture concept combine to make it a great idea. The first is its universalism: all men have cultures, and this helps define their common humanity. Second is a focus on organization: all cultures show coherence and structure, ranging from universal patterns common among all human lifeways (for instance, every culture includes marriage rules) to the peculiar designs of specific times and places (such as particular ways of managing monogamy or polygamy). Third is a recognition of man's creativity: each culture is a collective product of human effort, feeling, and thought. Taken together, these conceptions represent much of the anthropological response to our awareness of astonishing differences among mutually exotic groups of mankind, their works, and their ways. The concept of culture makes all these varied patterns intelligible as collective systems created, and continually being re-created, by human beings living ordered group existences. Thus on the one hand each way of life is seen as a unique human contribution, worthy of respect by virtue of its very existence, valid in terms of the experience of those who made it and those who live by it. Yet at the same time each set of lifeways, despite its singularity, becomes intelligible as one member of the total class of phenomena known as cultures.

So the initial mixed responses of wonder, contempt, fear, and romanticism as Western man faced the universe of cultural variety have been replaced—or at least contained and moderated—by a reasoned conception. This is a conception with firm intellectual foundations in scholarship and science. It also has deep roots in humanist philosophy and humanitarian values. The idea of culture has been a most important weapon in the intellectual attack against racism, ethnocentrism, bigotry, and cultural imperialism. It has been among the sources of many progressive and enlightened public attitudes and social policies in modern times. In an otherwise tragic world conducive to pessimism for the humanist, the implications and potentialities of the culture idea can be a source of hope, from both scholarly and ideological points of view.

Within these broad significances and connotations, the term culture also conveys quite precise meanings. Strictly speaking, the word is far from having a single meaning agreed upon by everyone who uses it. Among the human sciences alone one finds many technical differences in usage. Indeed, whole volumes have been devoted to comparing and evaluating different scholarly concepts and definitions of culture. Moreover, these differences are not all minuscule or negligible. Some of them reflect disagreements between schools of thought about the very nature of culture. Nevertheless, there is a long-standing consensus on the core of meaning denoted by the term. This general agreement is most widespread among cultural anthropologists, though it is extensively recognized outside anthropology as well. It is the nucleus of meaning established by this consensus that will be referred to throughout this book as the anthropological concept of culture.

Culture in this sense has come to mean, most simply, the entire way of life followed by a people. The bearers of a culture are understood to be a collectivity of individuals such as a society or a community. One important implication of this formulation is that culture and society are not the same, though of course they are closely related. The cultural patterns that shape the behavior of people in groups should not be confused with the structure of institutions or social systems, even though each is obviously dependent on the other. A classical anthropological definition of culture is "that complex whole which includes knowledge, belief, art, morals, laws, customs, and any other capabilities and habits acquired by man as a member of society."[1] A more modern definition refers to the "organization of experience" shared by members of a community, including "their standards for perceiving, predicting, judging, and acting."[2] This means that culture includes all socially standardized ways of seeing and thinking about the world; of understanding relationships among people, things, and events; of establishing preferences and purposes; of carrying out actions and pursuing goals. In a general sense, then, culture consists of the rules which generate and guide behavior. More specifically, the culture of a particular people or other social body is everything that one must learn to behave in ways that are recognizable, predictable, and understandable to those people.

The positive descriptions of virtues inherent in the culture concept given earlier in this discussion should not be allowed to inflate its value. Let it be understood that this concept is only one among many that are very important in the study of human behavior; it has its own limitations and weaknesses; it can be and has been misused by anthropologists and others. The idea of culture is no more important than other master concepts of group life such as society, community, power, or inequality. Like these others, culture is a rather broad, general concept. With some notable exceptions such as language, most aspects of culture have proved difficult to describe with great precision or economy of expression. Some of the research methods required to study cultures resist standardization or precise replication, and many scientists see this as a serious difficulty. Students of culture often face a difficult problem in making large amounts of factual evidence intelligible in terms of meaningful parts and processes of cultural systems. The label culture has sometimes been applied to quite generalized, loose, even vague descriptions of social life. Such misuses need not concern us here, except when they occur in studies of poverty and the poor.

There is a branch of anthropology appropriately called *social* rather than cultural anthropology. Social anthropologists have generally treated the culture concept in ways that are different from its use in cultural anthropology. They have typically been interested in social relations and social institutions rather than culture. Many have used this concept little or not at all in their analyses of social systems. Some treat culture as synonymous with society. Others give it a more restricted meaning corresponding to values and beliefs or other patterns which would be regarded as only part of culture according to the consensus of cultural anthropology outlined earlier. One school of thought within social anthropology has been highly influential in the study of the American class system. The founder of this school, W. Lloyd Warner, has written: "Culture [is] usually used as a synonym for society, the subject matter of the ethnologist or social anthropologist. . . ." "Social anthropologists are essentially comparative sociologists. They attempt to discover the nature of society and to understand better any one type of society by a comparative study of the several types found throughout the world."[3] Through their earlier studies of social classes in American communities this group of scholars has undoubtedly influenced some recent writings on poverty, including certain works to be discussed here in later chapters. In an exhaustive account of social science ideas about poverty these links would receive attention. The purpose of this book, however, is to develop a critical understanding of selected dominant conceptions in contemporary thought about culture and poverty. For this purpose it is sufficient to make clear that the frame of reference adopted by the "Warner school" makes it quite peripheral to the anthropological consensus on the nature of culture.

Some Insights of Cultural Theory

In developing the culture concept and using it to interpret many varieties of social existence, anthropologists and other scholars have clarified a number of basic issues underlying the human condition. One such insight is the recognition that through culture men collectively adapt themselves to environmental conditions and historical circumstances. Cultures have thus come to be understood as adaptive responses to such conditions and circumstances. Indeed, environing habitats and external historical influences are among the major kinds of factors that men cope with by means of their cultures.

This makes it understandable that the environmental resources available to any people and the human events stemming from other groups of men profoundly condition, stimulate, and limit the development of cultures. For example, contemporary Eskimo cultures include manifold adaptations both to the arctic habitat and to the developing European domination of the circumpolar region. Neither one of these sets of conditions was created by Eskimos, and neither one is part of the rules and standards which make up Eskimo cultures. Yet both these aspects of external reality have been conceptualized by Eskimo minds, dealt with through changing and developing indigenous lifeways, and thus have importantly conditioned the growth of modern Eskimo culture.

Some of the modern changes in this example have involved accepting elements from European cultural sources.

At the same time, Europeans living in the arctic have recognized the effectiveness of some Eskimo adaptations—rules for making and using appropriate types of clothing, shelter, and transportation—and adopted them. Moreover, Eskimos living by their traditional lifeways for many centuries in their native habitat have no doubt brought about changes (however slight) in the landscape and life forms of the natural environment. Yet none of these reciprocal adaptive relationships contradicts the fact that both material resources and human events from external sources are ultimately prior to, and therefore separate from, the culture of any human collectivity. When we come to consider the cultural adaptations of the poor in America and elsewhere, it will be necessary to keep these distinctions clear in that context as well.

Another insight stemming from the concept of culture is still too little understood outside anthropology, even in other human sciences. This is an understanding of the distinction and mutual relations between social statistics and cultural patterns. Ever since early attempts to understand relationships among kinsmen in exotic societies a century ago, it has gradually become clear that the statistics of social behavior are only one kind of raw data needed to portray and interpret cultural systems. A major source of this understanding has been the anthropological search for universalistic conceptions to establish order in the panhuman variety of social forms, particularly domestic and kinship groupings. In these and other connections it has now long been clear that census figures alone tell us nothing directly about structure or process in a cultural system. To the extent that census data are valid, they give us the statistical shape of a demographic reality. This statistical pattern is a surface phenomenon that may have a wide variety of cultural designs for living underlying it.

Consider, for example, a demographic pattern in which at any one time there are many households without an observable resident adult male heading the domestic menage. This picture may reflect a system of plural marriage in which co-wives reside separately and husbands live with one wife at a time, as is the case in polygynous societies in numerous parts of the world. It may reflect a community organization in which all adult males reside together and apart from their wives and children, as in much of the Southwest Pacific. It may be associated with a traditional family form in which male support for the household comes from kinsmen by blood, with no such social position as resident husband, as among the Nayar of South India. It may be found in societies where males are migrant laborers for periods of years while their spouses and offspring remain in the home community, as in many colonial areas. Or it may reflect a variety of systems in which multiple consensual unions involve males in various standardized obligations to women and children, not including cohabitation, as reported from Caribbean societies. Thus the census taker's finding by itself has no definite cultural significance but may turn out, with further investigation, to have many different meanings. The problem of relationships between census information and cultural forms will be highly relevant to much that has been written on the poor in America.

Another clarification involves the distinction between cultural values and situational or circumstantial adaptations. The values of a culture include the ideals, the aims and ends, the ethical and aesthetic standards, and the criteria of knowledge and wisdom embodied within it, taught to and modified by each human generation. These values are not simply manifested straightforwardly on the surface of everyday life; they are related to experience and behavior in complicated, variable, and indirect ways. What is prized and endorsed according to the standards of a cultural system is not always manifest or practically available in the exigencies of ongoing existence. Anthropologists therefore do not expect to find all the values that lend inner coherence to a way of life directly or overtly expressed in everyday life.

Our growing understanding of the part played by values in

cultural systems has thus helped to expose one of the crudities of conventional wisdom. This is the simple misconception that people everywhere live as they do because they prefer their actual mode of existence and its consequences. Indeed, there can be few human situations that allow full enactment of cultural values in the practical world. So we have come to suspect that either romantic ennoblement or unwarranted debasement of the subject is at work when a people's values are simply inferred directly from the surface aspects of their lives. That is, the picture of the noble savage and the portrayal of the happy slave are equally suspect as unrealistic projections.

Every culture both influences and reflects the world view of those who live by its rules. World views consist of shared perceptions informed by values. Yet the relationship of any world view to experience and to behavior is complex, subtle, and many-sided. It may well be true that "all values are situationally anchored,"[4] and it is certainly true that circumstances often demand that values be compromised or contradicted by situational adaptations. This may be related to the fact that different values within one system may have higher or lower priorities. Nevertheless, it seems probable that opportunities to choose goals, in accordance with value priorities or otherwise, are objectively narrowed when life chances in general are reduced by the structure of society. We shall consider below whether this is the case for the poor in highly stratified social systems like that of the United States.

METHODS OF STUDYING CULTURES

Consistent with these orientations to the world of cultural variety is the approach by which anthropologists generally have preferred to gain knowledge of any particular way of life. This is the form of field research known as ethnography. It requires that the ethnographer live with the people whose culture he studies. From the time of pioneer field workers onward, it has been recognized that prolonged, intensive, direct exposure to the actual conditions of life is needed to understand a previously unknown culture. This involves direct observation of social behavior and participation in community life as well as systematic questioning and discussion with informants. Only by this immersion in ongoing group existence can the anthropologist probe thoroughly beneath the surface of a culture and replace superficial impressions with more accurate insights. While he knows that he must ultimately remain an alien, the ethnographer must nevertheless strive to combine his outsider's perception with an insider's view of the culture. This in essence is how the anthropologist discovers the order and design that give coherence to a way of life; this is how he discerns the articulation between a culture and the environmental and historical conditions to which it is an adaptation; it is by these means that he lays bare the structure and processes underlying social statistics; and it is thus that he finds a value system behind the surfaces and circumstances of everyday life.

Among the sources of ethnographic method was a keenly felt need to overcome the limitations of other observers who often preceded the anthropologist in describing life among alien and exotic peoples: explorers, conquerors, traders, missionaries, and imperial administrators. With few exceptions, the observations of these men were necessarily external and superficial. Moreover, it was inherent in their viewpoint that they should see social order mainly in whatever they could discern that seemed analogous to Western institutions and patterns. To them, more often than not, all else was either bestial savagery or natural—i.e., cultureless—nobility. Because of their role in the process of culture contact these observers are necessarily culture-bound and ethnocentric. One of the sources of tension remaining to this day between anthropologists and these men is that a good ethnographer simply cannot accept descriptions or evaluations of a local way of life by colonial administrators and missionaries as sufficient or necessarily valid evidence. As we shall see, there are analogous problems in the study of the poor in our own society today.

This approach to the essential task of obtaining basic information calls attention to another side of anthropology, and of the culture concept. While the anthropologist practices a comparative and generalizing science, he is also a specialist in the particular cultures he knows most intimately. Similarly, the universal idea of culture is matched by the quite particularistic conception of each specific way of life. There is neither contradiction nor paradox in this twofold approach. Indeed, it is by his very immersion in the specific distinctiveness of another way of life that the anthropologist frees himself from the preconceptions inherent in his own culture. Without this, his comparative discipline would be in danger of becoming a mere exercise in provincial comparison against the standards of his own way of life. This is of course precisely the popular error that anthropology is dedicated to overcoming.

In a sense, the ethnographer transcends his own ethnocentrism, which is an inevitable result of his nature as a cultural being, by temporarily entering into other culturally provincial worlds. By this approach he can discover the inner coherence of an alien or exotic culture with relative independence from the biases of his own cultural provenience. While this may be an ideal seldom fully realized, the anthropologist can approach the perspective of viewing a culture from within and in its own terms. This enables him to portray a non-Western way of life in such a way that it is intelligible without constant reference to direct comparison with Western patterns. Each such portrayal becomes one case of many upon which a comparative science and a universalistic culture concept are founded.

SOME PHILOSOPHICAL TENETS AND VALUES

These scholarly and scientific orientations of method and theory carry philosophical implications for questions of value judgment and ideological issues. Most obviously, perhaps, they imply that every existing culture is a valid human creation entitled to recognition and respect. Perhaps few workers in the human sciences would disagree with this statement, but agreement would probably be less universal on the additional implications suggested below. In my view, the conceptions reviewed here imply that we should be very cautious about absolute judgments of the superiority or inferiority of any cultural system in comparison with others. Beyond this, it can be argued that sufficient evidence has now accumulated to justify the assumption that any culture has the basic qualities of organization, pattern, and design—unless and until it is proved otherwise. The expectable exceptions to this generalization would be ways of life which have undergone such extremities of natural catastrophe, military conquest, or other destruction that they have disintegrated. Thus in order to demonstrate that any existing culture manifests disorganization or disorder as a prime characteristic, one would have to show that the way of life had lost its coherence through some such destructive process.

Next, our earlier considerations impose an obligation upon the describers and analyzers of any culture to distinguish carefully between cultural patterns and external conditions, whether environmental or historical. In particular, care must be taken not to hold those who live by a culture responsible or accountable for conditions that are beyond their control, including ineluctable restrictions or limitations imposed by unavoidable intergroup contacts. Similarly, it is incumbent upon those who use the culture concept not to confuse social statistics with culture patterns but to discover by independent investigation the patterns that underlie demographic data. This includes resisting the error of assuming that census information has the same cultural significance elsewhere that it might be assumed to have in conventional, middle-class Western communities. The foregoing considerations also mean that students of any way of life should refrain from imputing cultural values to it merely from the externals of social existence. In particular, an effort should be made to determine whether values may not exist that are prevented from realization and fulfillment by uncontrollable conditions of situational stress or limitation.

Finally, the concepts reviewed here imply that any student of a culture ought to make every effort to view that way of life from within and in terms of its own internal logic. That is, it is neither intellectually nor ethically acceptable to portray another way of life merely in terms of comparison, invidious or otherwise, with one's own cultural standards. This means that some reasonable equivalent of the ethnographic process sketched earlier must be carried out before a functioning cultural system can be presented either accurately or fairly. In my view, these implications of the culture concept, as it grew out of the meeting between Western man and the rest of humanity, help to make clear why this conception has been linked with humanitarian causes. Since this link constitutes one of the great values of the culture idea, students of culture and users of the concept should strive to preserve and strengthen this connection.

POVERTY AND INEQUALITY

The primary meaning of poverty is a condition of being in want of something that is needed, desired, or generally recognized as having value. A moment's reflection on such related concepts as indigence, penury, and destitution makes it clear that there are variable degrees of poverty. As the primary definition implies, poverty varies in terms of recognized values. Starvation, death from exposure, and loss of life due to some other total lack of resources are the only absolute forms of poverty. Even here we are dealing with only one end of a scale that extends toward a quite indefinite opposite extreme. Everyone knows that being poor in the United States means something different from being poor in India; the same is true of America in the 1960's compared with the 1930's or another decade. Among the more obvious differences are the total amounts of consumable resources available in relation to the population, the distribution of control over resources within the social structure, the cultural standards of value and adequacy, the proportion of the society's membership whose level of disposable resources stands below such standards, and the degree of contrast in welfare between higher and lower socioeconomic strata.

The state of poverty is thus a continuum rather than a point on an absolute scale. The condition is always defined in relation to a variety of quantitative and qualitative criteria which change as societies and cultures change. In the last few years much energy and effort have been expended in the United States to establish income criteria and other standards of poverty, then to count the poor on the basis of the resulting definitions, and so to assess the magnitude and dimensions of the sociopolitical problems presented by poverty. Much information has thus been gathered that is useful for a variety of purposes. Spirited debates have arisen over how many poor people exist, who and where they are, and related issues. Scholars and politicians alike have recently rediscovered the utility of phrases like "the invisible poor" and "the uncounted poor." Poverty expands and contracts, and its definition changes in accordance with temporary exigencies, including the interests of those who propound the definitions and do the counting.

The idea of poverty is above all a comparative concept that refers to a relative quality. For this reason no concrete definition will be offered here, though conceptions worked out by others will be taken into account below. As a quality, however, the condition of being poor does have a central significance: the essence of poverty is inequality. In slightly different words, the basic meaning of poverty is relative deprivation. The poor are deprived in comparison with the comfortable, the affluent, and the opulent. The kind of privation that first comes to mind with the word poverty is inequality of material wealth. Other insufficiencies are no doubt always correlated with material want, though in varying combinations from one society to another. In the contemporary United States, it is generally recognized that the poor are disadvantaged in a number of other areas widely agreed to be of value: occupations, education, and political power among others. Desired resources in each of these areas of life are quite unevenly distributed among the several strata of the American class system. At the same time, however, American ideological values assign great importance to equality. This inconsistency is a fundamental aspect of the cultural context of poverty as a social problem in the United States. For this reason the definition of poverty as inequality is perhaps particularly appropriate to the American scene.

Since being poor in many societies is closely associated with status in a hierarchy of social classes, poverty has often been studied as an aspect of class systems. These systems themselves are of course major structural expressions of inequality. It is not necessary here to go into the complex technical question how social classes are defined. It appears that by the cultural standards of contemporary American society all families and individuals of the lower class are among the poor, and some relatively disadvantaged members of the working class may also be regarded as poor.

CONTRADICTIONS OF THE POVERTY CULTURE CONCEPT

Today we are witnessing another great human confrontation, comparable in some ways to that which produced the modern idea of culture. In the mid-twentieth century, the more privileged and comfortable strata of Western society are finding themselves confronted as never before by the poor at the bottom of their social order. While present interest tends to focus on this confrontation as it occurs within the developed societies of the West, particularly the United States, this is becoming a universal phenomenon as the modern, urban, industrial social order becomes worldwide.

As a result of this new situation, there is again a demand for systematic knowledge about groups or categories of humanity to which relatively little attention was previously given. Again, there is also a need for concepts to render this knowledge coherent and to help shape both public attitudes and public policy. The principal result so far is the well-known idea of a "culture of poverty." Though less well known popularly, similar and closely related conceptions abound in the technical literature: "lower-class culture"; "low-income life styles"; "lower-class Negro culture"; "culture of unemployment"; "culture of the uninvolved"; "culture of violence"; "slum culture"; and even "dregs culture." Indeed, as we shall see later (chapter 5, pp. 104–7), these labels are part of what amounts to an intellectual fad of attributing a "culture" or "subculture" to almost any social category.

None of these phrases refers to an idea of seminal importance like the concept of culture itself. They all represent attempts to extend the application of that concept. Moreover, they are all misapplications of the original concept. A major thesis of this essay is that the culture-of-poverty notion and related ideas contradict all important positive aspects of the culture concept. This thesis of contradiction extends not only to the essential meaning of the idea of culture but also to its major implications for theory and method in the human sciences, philosophical issues, public attitudes, and public policies. While one assumes that the purposes of the authors involved were quite otherwise, the presentation and particularly the popularization of these notions have had one outstandingly important effect. That is, these formulations support the long-established rationalization of blaming poverty on the poor. Nothing could be further from the meaning, the spirit, or the ideological implications of the original concept of culture.

It is not my thesis that cultural distinctions confined to the poor are either impossible in principle or necessarily nonexistent in fact. On the contrary, considerable attention will be given in later pages to the problem of discovering what kinds of cultural designs do animate the existence of those who live in poverty. It will be shown, however, that presently available conceptions of poverty culture stand very much in the way of solving that factual problem. These conceptions are essentially prejudgments of empirical questions. Judgments inevitably involve values. It is the associated social values which make the conceptions discussed here especially relevant to problems of public policy.

CRITIQUES AND ALTERNATIVE CONCEPTS

The attribution of a distinctive cultural system to the poor has been widely accepted and indeed seems increasingly to be taken for granted. At the same time, however, there has been a certain amount of criticism and opposition. Alternative interpretations of life under conditions of poverty have not been entirely lacking. Much of the behavior alleged to be specifically characteristic of the lower class, and therefore often invoked as evidence of cultural distinctiveness, has been explained on other grounds. For example, the correlation between poverty and crime has been interpreted as the outcome of a social structure combining unequal opportunity for different strata with the same success goals for all. This interpretation not only omits any reference to a "culture of poverty" but explicitly rests upon the finding that significant cultural values are shared by different social strata. Critics of the general looseness with which the culture concept is often employed in this context have followed this up by arguing that such usage frequently involves a conceptual confusion between culture and class.

Most of the critical questions that have been raised are related in one way or another to this central issue of the relationship between culture and social class. It has been suggested that lower-class life is more variable and heterogeneous than common uses of the culture concept indicate. It has been shown that analysis in terms of the "culture of poverty" may distract attention from crucial structural characteristics of the stratified social system as a whole and focus it instead on alleged motivational peculiarities of the poor that are of doubtful validity or relevance. Several investigations of the problem of class cultures suggest that the cultural values of the poor may be much the same as middle-class values, merely modified in practice because of situational stresses. The view has been presented that such putative lower-class characteristics as self-indulgence or inability to defer gratification are better explained by situational variables than by determinants of class affiliation.

Some anthropologists and sociologists have felt that much social scientific research and writing about the life of the poor is biased by a middle-class point of view. A series of papers delivered at the 1966 meeting of the American Anthropological Association shows how the "culture of poverty" notion and associated ideas distort the reality of life among the poor, prejudice our understanding of that life, and encourage policies which perpetuate the disadvantages associated with poverty. All these critiques and alternatives are valuable, and they all deserve attention. This book owes something to each of them.

2 The Self-perpetuating Lower Class: A Cultural Image and Its National Policy Reflections

We are concerned here with doctrines that point to presumed defects in the mentality or behavior of disadvantaged classes, then go on to explain their social position and deprivation as resulting from these internal deficiencies. There is of course a long philosophical evolution behind the modern emergence of these doctrines. That history cannot be traced here. The contemporary American manifestation of this evolving orientation has its immediate roots in the intellectual history of the past twenty years. Following World War II, a number of important reorientations developed in the human sciences, social criticism, and public policies. The essence of these changes has recently been approvingly chronicled by a social thinker who was instrumental in bringing about the process he describes.

> And, as a matter of fact, the next turn in the development of social research in this area tended to support [Franklin Frazier's view of lower-class life as "all bad"]. For the period of lower-class romanticization came to an end under the double impact of change in society and change in social science—and there is no question that the first was more important. The change in society was heralded by the explosion of independence movements in colonial areas. . . . Thus the cultural relativistic stance in sociology and anthropology went into eclipse. The question now was: How do we get development? And social scientists followed suit, now picking up their leads from Weber as well as Freud and searching for backgrounds that emphasized ambition, achievement, work, aspiration. In this perspective, of course, the lower-class family came out rather badly—it was

studied only as a mine of potential raw materials, some of which might be fashioned into the psychological material useful for achievement. . . .

And, meanwhile, our own colonial problem rose in seriousness to become the major domestic issue in American life. Just as the cultures and psychologies of the peoples of the world were now studied from the point of view of determining how they might be made more equal economically and politically, so we began in a fragmentary way to study the culture and psychology of lower-class Negroes from the same point of view: What obstacles to equality are presented?[1]

The significance of this passage lies as much in its context as in its content. It appears in the Preface, by a major contemporary sociologist, to a new edition of a classic in Negro sociology largely devoted to the lower-class family and originally published nearly thirty years ago. Much of the material found in the more recent literature on the "culture of poverty" and "lower-class culture" is prefigured in this, *The Negro Family in the United States*, and other respected works by E. Franklin Frazier. Glazer's respectful Preface is a revealing gloss on this relationship, for much of what he has to say emphasizes how modern Frazier's approach seems to him, and how Frazier would have approved of current trends.

Glazer makes the ideological underpinnings and the value position of this orientation perfectly explicit when he approvingly paraphrases a judgmental passage from Frazier.

The Negro is applauded for surviving in a society based on laissez faire and competition, for his strivings, for the curbing of individual desires and impulses, for assimilating a new mode of life [white middle-class patterns]. By contrast of course his failure to strive and to curb his impulses would be seen as *his* failure rather than society's failure, though society—history—would certainly have to share a good part of the blame [italics in the original].[2]

All this takes on further significance when one recognizes that much of the recent writing on "lower-class culture" comes from studies of the Negro American poor. It is also significant that the Frazierian tradition of moralistic denigration of the lower class is prominently perpetuated in the writings of Glazer himself and one of his collaborators, Daniel P. Moynihan.

THE PEJORATIVE TRADITION ESTABLISHED BY
E. FRANKLIN FRAZIER

In the work of Frazier there are many contributions to the developing idea of class culture. Chief among these is the theme of disorganization in the life of the urban black poor. This image is developed virtually to the point of denying that the Negro masses in American cities live by any coherent cultural system at all. Frazier mourns what he calls the "Passing of the Gentleman and the Peasant." Under this heading he tells us, "There have been only two really vital cultural traditions in the social history of the Negro in the United States: one being the genteel tradition of a small group of mulattoes who assimilated the morals and manners of the slaveholding aristocracy; and the other, the culture of the [rural] black folk who gave the world the Spirituals."[3] In Frazier's view these were genuine cultures, but they were things of the past. As for the Black Bourgeoisie made famous by Frazier, he portrayed their way of life in no uncertain terms as what Edward Sapir called a spurious culture. Frazier describes existence among the modern Negro poor as an immoral chaos brought about by disintegration of the black folk culture under the impact of urbanization. In the end, the only cultural validity Frazier grants to modern Negro Americans is, as he puts it, "taking on the [middle-class] folkways and mores of the white race."[4]

Within this context Frazier creates an image of the black poor as so abysmally disorganized and so hopelessly infected with social pathologies that they even lack public opinion, social control, or community institutions. This appears to be a major source of one of the most prominent and logically confused themes in the later conceptions of "lower-class culture" and the "culture of poverty." While these constructs are labeled and treated as "cultures," they are nevertheless presented as so lacking in basic elements of organization universal among human lifeways that they stand quite outside any usual definition of the term culture. Thus life in the culture of the poor takes on the paradoxical meaning of life without culture, or at least without major elements previously understood as necessary aspects of culture.

The hyperbole of these images can be illustrated by a few representative lines from one of Frazier's best-known works.

Family desertion has been one of the inevitable consequences of the urbanization of the Negro population . . . it appears from available sources of information that desertions are more frequent in the Negro families than in the families of other racial groups. . . .

In many cases these broken families were once well adjusted to the simple rural southern community . . . The behavior of Negro deserters, who are likely to return to their families even after several years of absence, often taxes the patience of social workers whose plans for their families are constantly disrupted . . . poverty, ignorance, and color force them to such homes in deteriorated slum areas from which practically all institutional life has disappeared. Hence at the same time that simple rural families are losing their internal cohesion, they are being freed from the controlling force of public opinion and communal institutions. . . .

It is impossible to draw any conclusions from available statistics concerning either the volume or the trend of illegitimacy among Negroes . . . illegitimacy is from five to ten times as high among Negroes as among whites. . . .

Undoubtedly, much of the illegitimacy issues from social disorganization and results in personal demoralization. . . . During the course of their migration to the city, family ties are broken, and the restraints which once held in check immoral sex conduct lose their force.[5]

The major evidence on which this portrayal is based is of four kinds: official census data, statistical reports of social service agencies, records from the police and the courts, and case histories from social workers. Each of these may be a legitimate and useful source of information when analyzed in the context of other data and evaluated against other sources. Taken alone, however, these forms of information not only are woefully inadequate but may be quite misleading. Frazier's misuse of census data as direct evidence of "social disorganization" glaringly violates the student of culture's distinction between statistical patterns and cultural configurations. The same difficulty is inherent in Frazier's use of other statistical data as well.

Frazier shows little or no awareness of the built-in biases that must be suspected as affecting all information from social workers, service agencies, police, and courts. Each of these sources is confined, by its own cultural definition and social function, to focusing its attention on behavior and social phenomena that are conventionally defined as "disorganized." These phenomena are therefore assumed, without reference to observation, to be disorderly and deviant. Indeed, these professionals are such specialists in "disorganization" that they do not know what to do with conduct they would otherwise call organized behavior, when it occurs where they do not expect it. Frazier presents a telling if unwitting commentary when he remarks that it "taxes the patience" of these paternalistic functionaries when "deserters" return to their families. These observers from the service professions are trained to identify order and organization with conformity to conventional middle-class or "stable working-class" norms. Any possibility of finding another kind of social organization or cultural patterning in observations from these sources is confounded from the outset. The reports of life among the poor emanating from policemen, judges, and welfare workers are the domestic equivalent of portrayals and assessments of indigenous lifeways by colonial administrators or missionaries. They are no more acceptable as valid data, without being checked against independent evidence, than their analogues in this other context.

This makes it all the more significant that any depiction of ongoing social existence in a human population is conspicuously missing from Frazier's work. The reader does not get the feeling that the author has observed the life of slum dwellers intensively at firsthand, much less participated in that life. Thus materials against which his main data might be evaluated are not presented. Filtered case histories and statistical abstractions cannot make up for this. From these difficulties flow contradictions and even absurdities. In one of his more cautious passages Frazier tells us that "no conclusions" about volume or trend can be drawn from statistics on illegitimacy. Yet two pages later we are informed without qualification that illegitimacy is five or ten times higher among Negroes than among whites. Then come the sweeping and extreme statements that "all institutional life has disappeared" and slum dwellers are "freed from the controlling force of public opinion." The credibility of the entire portrait seems very much open to question in the absence of any further evidence to substantiate such drastic descriptions.

An essential element in Frazier's reasoning is one that is perpetuated by later thinkers. This is a direct logical leap from social statistics, which are deviant in terms of middle-class norms, to a model of disorder and instability. Such reasoning effectively eliminates consideration of possible cultural forms that, in spite of differing from Frazier's assumed standard, might have their own order and functions. For example, an implicit assumption is continually evident that female family heads receive no significant support from any social network. Yet there is no indication of the careful study that would be required to determine whether or not female-headed households maintain functional relationships with nonresident male consorts, maternal or paternal kinsmen, other relatives by blood or marriage, or indeed any other sources of support except welfare agencies.

Frazier, like his successors, fails to follow up leads in his data that might help to clarify issues otherwise glossed over. The reader searches in vain for any investigation into the role of the temporarily absent males who upset social workers by returning to their families. Have these men been in communication with the households to which they return? Are they links in a wider network? Or what? Frazier does not attend to such empirical questions, preferring instead to cover everything with the blanket concept of disorganization. It is difficult to avoid the impression that this conceptualization admits only two possibilities: order on a conventional middle-class model, or disorder.

The same impression is fostered by Frazier's free use of value-laden terminology, ranging from his romantic and condescending picture of "simple peasant folk" to his vigorous condemnation of "immoral sex conduct" in a "vicious environment." This is not the usual vocabulary of a scientist attempting to order social reality. Nor is it the language of a sensitive observer portraying human beings for whom he has developed either empathy or sympathy. On the contrary, Frazier projects his own commitment to the values of a middle-class professional and his disapproval of what he perceives as contradictions of these values by the urban Negro poor. Indeed, one comes to suspect that "social disorganization" is little more than an academic-sounding label for behavior which Franklin Frazier feels is contrary to his own value system. Meanwhile we have learned little about whether the lives of the people in question are organized in any empirically verifiable sense. One suspects that, for Frazier, this is really not an issue at all. It is rather a matter of class-bound prejudgment.

THE NON-MELTING POT OF NATHAN GLAZER AND DANIEL P. MOYNIHAN

The Frazierian pejorative tradition of class culture has been forcefully perpetuated and extended by such contemporary scholars as Nathan Glazer and Daniel Patrick Moynihan. This may be seen in the recent book, *Beyond the Melting Pot*, on which these two authors collaborated. While this is ostensibly a study of ethnic minorities in New York City, many of its sources are national in scope, as are many of its generalizations and conclusions. Approximately one-fifth of this book is devoted to Negroes, and it is here that the Frazier tradition appears most explicitly, in a chapter written by Glazer. Little new evidence is reported here; recent research on New York Negroes was not yet available. The chapter is thus based on selections from the sparse descriptive literature available, plus scattered citations of interpretive writing with broader frames of reference. Nevertheless, this work is full of interpretations and judgments that are very much part of the Frazier tradition. For example, a recital of the familiar household and related statistics, updated by reference to the 1960 census, is followed by this passage.

> Broken homes and illegitimacy do not necessarily mean poor upbringing and emotional problems. But they mean it more often when the mother is forced to work (as the Negro mother so often is), when the father is incapable of contributing to support (as the Negro father so often is), when fathers and mothers refuse to accept responsibility for and resent their children, as Negro parents, overwhelmed by difficulties, so often do, and when the family situation, instead of being clear-cut, and with defined roles and responsibilities, is left vague and ambiguous (as it so often is in Negro families).[6]

The only sources given for the demographic evidence cited are the U.S. Census and a statistical study published by the Community Council of Greater New York. Frazier's book is cited as "the classical work" on "the general background of

Negro family life." The only other reference is to Hylan
Lewis, not as a source of any information set forth by Glazer,
but simply as "a recent perceptive review." No source or reference is specified for the judgmental interpretation set forth in
the paragraph quoted above.

Glazer devotes several pages to housing and neighborhood
patterns among New York Negroes. The principal descriptive source cited for this part of the chapter is the work of
McEntire. Glazer's discussion includes an analysis of the
effects of public housing projects on Negro slums. That
analysis forms the context for the following quotation.

> Large numbers of normal families living in slums (the chief
> candidates for the projects) have been withdrawn from them,
> leaving the remaining slums to become the homes of the old,
> the criminal, the mentally unbalanced, the most depressed and
> miserable and deprived. The slums now contain the very large
> families that are not eligible for public housing because they
> would overcrowd it; the families that have been ejected from the
> projects (or were never admitted) for being antisocial; those
> who have either recently arrived in the city and hardly adapted
> to urban life, or those who may have been here a long time but
> never adapted; as well as the dope peddlers and users, the sex
> perverts and criminals, the pimps and prostitutes whom the
> managers reject or eject to protect the project population. All
> these are now concentrated in the slums that ring the projects,
> and areas that were perhaps just barely tolerable before the
> impact of the projects are now quite intolerable. As we tear
> down the slums, those that remain inevitably become worse.
> And what after all are we to do with the large numbers of peo-
> ple emerging in modern society who are irresponsible and de-
> praved? The worthy poor create no serious problem—nothing
> that money cannot solve. But the unworthy poor? No one has
> come up with the answers.[7]

Here we see the difficulties and weaknesses of Frazier's approach still manifest despite a generation of progress in sociological sophistication. The principal sources of information
in this study of urban Negroes are essentially the same as in

earlier research. Despite the continuing inadequacy of these sources, the same sort of analysis and interpretation, going well beyond the data, is still presented. The same confusion between demography and social structure continues to be evident. One still finds nonconformity with middle-class norms uncritically equated with instability and disorganization. Pejorative moralism remains a prominent theme. One still searches in vain for any integrated portrayal of life among the people in question.

Moreover, the vigor with which disorganization is imputed to Negroes, and the harshness with which it is condemned, stand out in contrast to the treatment of other ethnic groups in this book, presumably because the authors see Negroes as more disorganized than the others. Similar social statistics on Puerto Rican households are treated more gently. One would hardly know from this work that groups other than Negroes lived in slums. Indeed, the entire entry under "Slums" in the Index reads, "*See* Negroes, housing." The chapters on Puerto Ricans, Jews, Italians, and Irish contain no despairing comments about the "irresponsible," "depraved," "unworthy poor." To some extent at least, this contrast seems related to indications in Glazer and Moynihan's source notes that more descriptive cultural material was available to them on the other groups than on Negroes. Thus once again it appears evident that sweeping generalizations, invidious comparisons, and harsh value-judgments come most easily in the absence of concrete knowledge or experience of the shape and dynamics of ongoing social existence.

Like Frazier before him and others since, Glazer is explicit about the causes he sees underlying the sad condition of the black lower class, and he has consistent advice to give in the realm of policy. Slavery and urbanization are treated as the principal destructive historical forces. Past discrimination in employment, education, and other fields receives full mention, while present discrimination is referred to more fleetingly. The major emphasis, however, is placed on such alleged

causes as "incapacity for business" and lack of achievement
in education. "The major part" of the cause for educational
underachievement is unhesitatingly ascribed to "the home
and family and community." While this is of course a very
popular conclusion—indeed now almost a ruling assumption
in much popular and official thinking—it has nevertheless
been vigorously challenged in recent years on the basis of
serious research. (See chapter 4, pp. 78–84.)

The prescription for the ills of the black lower class which
emerges from Glazer and Moynihan's analysis is predictably
patronizing and moralistic: self-help and self-examination.

> A new phase in Negro leadership must begin. . . . The era of the
> leaders of "protest" has been in full swing . . . but it is now
> entering an era of diminishing returns . . . there are as a matter
> of fact few additional gains to be made in New York City by
> protest. . . . Succeeding . . . the period of protest, one can de-
> tect the need for a period of self-examination and self-help, in
> which the increasing income and resources of leadership of the
> group are turned inwards.[8]

Earlier, however, these authors had diagnosed the social
pathology of the poor as so serious that it is beyond successful
therapy. "The magnitude of the problems in the lower class
and disorganized sector of the population is so great that the
middle-class element is inadequate to deal with them." Their
conclusion is that "it is not likely that we will see a massive
self-help effort."[9] Thus the principal causes of the plight of
the poor are found in the internal deficiencies of their own way
of life, and their total condition is seen as not only self-perpetuating, but essentially hopeless. Nevertheless, the authors
persist in offering condescending and moralizing advice, even
after they themselves have predicted that this advice will not
or cannot be followed. Such is the conceit of a self-conscious
elite, in scholarly guise, dispensing its wisdom to those whom
it holds responsible for what it has defined as "the unworthy
poor."

BUILDING THE FRAZIER TRADITION INTO NATIONAL POLICY: MOYNIHAN AGAIN

A more recent extension of the Frazierian vision of the lower class has become more important than earlier examples because it was primarily a vehicle for political intervention in public affairs. Indeed, this work succeeded, albeit briefly, in setting important aspects of the policy of the United States government toward a large proportion of the poor in America. The central document in this episode is the so-called "Moynihan Report." This slim volume became the basis for a Presidential speech establishing new federal policy goals, set off an extraordinary series of critical reactions, and led to a sizable semipublic national political wrangle. Evidently the major source of the controversy was that the "lower-class culture" thesis had been injected into the highest councils of public policy making. This made the class-culture idea an issue in the struggle for national social change represented by the civil rights movement. Certainly the substantive content of the Report was not in itself responsible for the great interest and contention, since there was nothing new in this.

Indeed, this document contains very little more than another updated rehash of Frazier, quite similar in all essentials of method and message to Moynihan's collaborative work with Glazer two years earlier. The substantive thesis is stated dramatically.

> At the heart of the deterioration of the fabric of Negro society is the deterioration of the Negro family. It is the fundamental source of weakness of the Negro community at the present time. . . . The white family has achieved a high degree of stability and is maintaining that stability. By contrast, the family structure of lower class Negroes is highly unstable, and in many urban centers is approaching complete breakdown.[10]

This is followed by all the familiar demographic data on households—"dissolved" marriages, illegitimacy, welfare rates, ADC figures, and so forth. Frazier is extensively quoted and

cited on the historical sources and sociological explanations
for these problems. From these sources Moynihan paints
with bold strokes a lower-class "subculture" highlighted by
"matriarchy," emasculated males, educational failure, delinquency, crime, and drug addiction.

Moynihan's reasoning from this diagnosis to policy implications is essentially direct and simple. This reasoning is summarized on the first page of the Report.

> The United States is approaching a new crisis in race rela-
> tions . . . in this period the expectations of the Negro Ameri-
> cans will go beyond civil rights. Being Americans, they will now
> expect that in the near future equal opportunities for them as a
> group will produce roughly equal results, as compared with
> other groups. This is not going to happen. Nor will it happen
> for generations to come unless a new special effort is made.
> . . . The harsh fact is that as a group, at the present time,
> in terms of ability to win out in the competitions of American
> life, they are not equal to most of those groups with which they
> will be competing. Individually, Negro Americans reach the
> highest peaks of achievement. But collectively, . . . Negroes are
> among the weakest . . . the circumstances of the Negro Ameri-
> can community in recent years have probably been getting
> *worse, not better* . . . the fundamental problem, in which this
> is most clearly the case, is that of family structure . . . so long
> as this situation persists, the cycle of poverty and disadvantage
> will continue to repeat itself.
> The thesis of this paper is that these events, in combination,
> confront the nation with a new kind of problem. Measures that
> have worked in the past, or would work for most groups in the
> present, will not work here. A national effort is required that
> will give a unity of purpose to the many activities of the Federal
> government in this area, directed to a new kind of goal: the
> establishment of a stable Negro family structure.[11]

It must be made clear that neither this document nor the
resultant Presidential speech contained any proposal for a
concrete program of action to implement the declared objectives. As far as public policy is concerned, both pieces are

limited to recommendations or declarations of rather general aims. Late in 1965 Moynihan published an article in which he briefly mentioned the family-allowance schemes of Europe and Canada, though he did not specifically recommend that the United States adopt similar programs. The same article also contains the following passage.

In itself, a national family policy need not be any more complex than were the provisions of the Employment Act of 1946. The point is not what answers are provided, but what questions are posed. The Employment Act said nothing about how to achieve the fullest measure of employment, but rather declared that the national government should be continually concerned with just that question, and should be constantly seeking answers.[12]

Even in early 1967 when Rainwater and Yancey published their very full and sympathetic account of the Report and the controversy, they pointed to no specific proposed action program. Thus for the period of active controversy at any rate, the upshot was a vague but apparently important shift in public policy goals, which focused federal attention and interest, in the broad field of race relations and poverty, upon Negro family structure. This shift must of course be related to the context of Moynihan's emphasis on internal weaknesses within the Negro community.

With this association, it is hardly surprising that civil rights leaders and Negro partisans suspected an effort to divert national energies from existing or projected programs for change in the total national social structure. Some already suspected that federal enforcement of recently enacted guarantees of employment opportunities and voting rights would not be vigorous. Others were preparing initiatives for more radical programs to deal with the interrelated problems of discrimination and poverty. The policy initiative associated with the Moynihan Report had many features that made it look rather like a diversionary tactic, designed to head off the necessity of confronting these rising problems. Most importantly, it tended to direct attention away from what the rest of society was still doing to the black poor, focusing instead on what the Negro lower class was allegedly doing to itself through its own defective and disabling "culture."

Much of the argument precipitated by the Moynihan Report has concerned the issue of the relationship between family form and other factors external to the family, including some variables with causes outside lower-class life altogether. Moynihan himself has been somewhat obscure about this, both in print and in public appearances, but the central thrust of his argument seems clear from a careful examination of his recent writings. The Report adduces statistical evidence that rising unemployment and falling family income are positively correlated with increasing divorce, higher ADC rates, and other indices of "family instability," up to 1960. Moynihan's inference seems to be that until 1960 the economic indicators reflected causes leading to results represented by the family statistics. Indeed, in one of his latest publications he writes of "the way in which unemployment, in particular, had controlled family stability and welfare dependency."[13]

Since 1960, Moynihan seems to argue, the deterioration of the family, together with all that supposedly depends on this, has continued with an independent impetus of its own. The empirical support for this suggestion to which Moynihan seems to attach most importance is the finding that between 1960 and 1964 unemployment declined slightly while the number of new ADC cases opened continued to rise. This is maintained in spite of the opposing fact that during the same years other "family" statistics, such as marital separation figures, continued to parallel employment trends much as they had before. Moynihan's formulation of independent family disintegration also ignores other evidence of ongoing economic deterioration in his own Report, such as the continued decline of Negro family income in relation to white income during the years in question.

In other words, there seems to be more evidence in the Moynihan Report itself to support the interpretation that changing household statistics respond to continuing economic forces, than to uphold the opposite interpretation. Nevertheless, Moynihan has erected a far-reaching thesis on this shaky basis, as the following quotations show.

> Obviously not every instance of social pathology afflicting the Negro community can be traced to the weakness of family structure. . . . Nonetheless, at the *center* of the tangle of pathology is the weakness of the family structure. Once or twice removed, it will be found to be *the principal source* of most of the aberrant, inadequate, or anti-social behavior that did not establish but now serves to *perpetuate the cycle* of poverty and deprivation [italics added].

And in his final summing up:

> What then is the problem? We feel that the answer is clear enough. Three centuries of injustice have brought about deep-seated structural distortions in the life of the Negro American. At this point, the present tangle of pathology is capable of *perpetuating itself without assistance from the white world.* The cycle can be broken only if these distortions are set right [italics added].[14]

So we come back to the same essential contention: whatever forces may have been at work in the past, today the main reason for the plight of the poor and the despised is the internal deficiencies in their own way of life.

My interpretation of the Moynihan Report as an attempt to inject the Frazierian concept of "lower-class culture" into national policy making—an interpretation based on the contents of the document itself—is strikingly confirmed by Moynihan's own published defense of the Report against his critics and opponents. Here he is explaining the purposes for which he wrote the Report:

> A word about these objectives: traditionally, the American legal and constitutional system has been based on a deliberate

blindness to any social reality other than the reality of individuals. . . . The reality of class had to be acknowledged. . . .
The report on the Negro family was intended to demonstrate
its relevance and thereby persuade the government that public
policy must now concern itself with issues beyond the frame of
individualistic political thinking.

The second objective was connected with and flowed from
the first . . . to win the attention of those in power. . . . It was
necessary to depict, and in terms that would be felt as well as
understood, the internal weakness of the Negro community and
the need for immense federal efforts. . . . Yet social indicators
such as these are relative, while family in a sense remains an
absolute: a broken family is broken; a deserted wife is alone;
an abandoned child needs help. Describing the plight of so
many Negro families appeared the surest way to bring home
the reality of their need. . . .

The plan of the Labor Department report was to pick up
from Frazier and record what had happened. As the data were
assembled . . . a compelling hypothesis began to emerge:
Frazier had been right [italics in the original].[15]

The opening sentence of the above quotation is of course
simply a historical and sociological absurdity: both class and
caste were built into the American legal and political systems
from the beginning. The remainder of this passage, however,
states with admirable clarity the relationships between scholarship, ideology, popular and official stereotypes, and political
tactics that had to be mobilized in order to bring the doctrine
of the "deviant subculture" to the center of the national
policy-making stage. These lines also communicate very directly just how far the proponents of class-culture ideas will
go in contradicting the whole concept of culture as it has
grown up in the human sciences, especially, it would seem,
when the political stakes are high. Nothing could be more
contrary to a whole sphere of understanding established by
students of culture than the statement that the family—
meaning of course the conventional middle-class Western
family—is absolute.

Ranged against this monumentally casual dismissal of the results of many decades spent in studying cultural variety in domestic groupings, Moynihan's other denials of elementary social science understanding seem paltry. Nevertheless, it should be noted that if there is anything that serious scholars of culture have learned, it is *not* to assume that a family is "broken" just because the official census records show no resident male heading the household; not to jump to the conclusion that a woman is "alone" merely because she appears on the census roles as "deserted"; or that a child has necessarily been "abandoned" just because a service agency reports that its father is absent. These passages reveal all too clearly that the purpose of such so-called social science, and the accompanying corruption of the culture concept, is not to illuminate human variety or to elucidate social reality. The purpose is rather to support a set of class-bound prejudgments about a troublesome element of our society. When these simplifications are presented as stratagems "to win the attention of those in power" by giving them something that can be "felt as well as understood," we are confronted with pseudo-scholarship used to good advantage in appealing to the ignorance and prejudices of the powerful.

It is not until the final paragraph of Moynihan's commentary on the Report and the attendant controversy that the last veil falls away to reveal openly what had previously only been implied.

There is no reason why Negroes need conform to anyone's standards but their own. . . . On the other hand, in order for this to be a *viable* position as well as a tenable one, it must reject not only conformity but dependency. . . . So long as exceptional numbers of Negro children are dependent on Welfare . . . and so long as vast numbers of Negro youth have to be helped along . . . Negroes will be at the mercy of whites demanding an end to "welfare chiseling" and "immorality." . . . If at the moment educated, middle-class Negroes are much in demand and doing nicely, this is not so for the lower class and

is likely never to be. This country is not fair to Negroes and
will exploit any weakness they display. Hence they simply cannot afford the luxury of having a large lower class that is at
once deviant *and* dependent. If they do not wish to bring it in
line with the working class . . . world around them, they must
devise ways to support it from within [italics in original].[16]

So in the end the seeming concern about victims of "social
pathology" falls away; the apparent humanitarian interest in
a social therapy for their ills is dropped. Ultimately the issue
is not stated in terms of collective health and welfare, but
rather in very blunt terms of conformity to be coerced by the
force of wealth and power. It is even admitted that what has
all along been described as inherently unhealthy and self-
destructive may be, on the contrary, perfectly tenable and entirely viable if only the lower class controlled more resources
than it does. This can only be described as a travesty of the
universalistic conceptions and humane values associated with
the idea of culture.

Here we find incautiously revealed the expedient attitude
toward the powerless underlying the political opportunism
that has been glorified and spuriously related to progressive
policy aims under the New Frontier slogan of "pragmatism"
and the Great Society shibboleth of "consensus." This callous
expression of middle-class willfulness, lying beneath pious
and pretentious words, gives force to the question whether
there is any hope for the black masses other than a vision of
Black Power somehow to be forged from their collective internal strength. And since this is more a class doctrine than a
racial dogma, these cold-blooded assertions of the power of
privilege raise anew the old question whether class warfare
and revolution may be the only salvation for the poor. Indeed, the implications of Moynihan's own prescriptions seem
to point in these directions. With unusual candor he tells the
poor that if they do not conform to "stable working class"
norms as defined by middle-class moralists like himself, they
will be coerced into a semblance of conformity and forcefully

punished for their deviations from respectability. Yet he offers no real program whereby the poor might gain access to the economic and political resources that are the wherewithal underlying acceptable lifeways among the organized working class and the affluent middle class. If it can be correctly assumed that this orientation is generally shared by the power-holding groups of contemporary society, it is fair to ask what alternative to the status quo exists for the poor. To what can they turn other than the classical class-conflict doctrines of the Old Left or the emerging group identity and action orientation of the New Left?

The harshness of Moynihan's position may have been somewhat softened, though its credibility as a basis for helping the poor was hardly enhanced, when he finally unveiled a plan to strengthen the family before a United States senatorial committee early in 1967. His presentation begins by briefly reiterating two of the most familiar and long-standing unimplemented commitments of establishment liberalism: "genuine full employment" plus "retraining and re-education." His third point and major recommendation, as forecast in earlier hints, is a federal program of family or children's allowances. This plan is modeled on contemporary Canadian and Scandinavian schemes, and it claims forebears in liberal American proposals going back more than forty years. The specifics are: $9 billion expended annually to provide amounts ranging from $8 per month for every child in the nation under six, up to $12 monthly for older dependents to age seventeen. This adds up to some $40 a month or $480 per year for an average family with four children. Note that these funds are by no means to be set aside for the poor. On the contrary, the proposal is to make equal payments to all children without exception, presumably on the theory that political realism requires removing any possible hint of positive discrimination in favor of the underprivileged.

Let us make the plausible assumption that no more than twenty-five per cent of the population is poor by income standards. This means that at least three-quarters of the annual expenditure, as proposed by Moynihan, would go to families ranging from those who need it relatively little to those who need it least. This amounts to passing off as aid to the poor a scheme whose main resources would actually go to people who already have adequate incomes, not to mention the rich. Moreover, it would work essentially like all other so-called "antidiscrimination" and "antipoverty" programs based on the spurious principles of "equal rights" and "equal opportunities" for people who start out with grossly unequal resources. That is, it would have no effect upon relative deprivation, which as we saw in chapter 1 is the central issue of poverty. Such a plan grants no relative advantage to the presently disadvantaged. This is thus one more of the many schemes for perpetuating the essence of the status quo while encouraging an unrealistic hope that the proportions of society's resources controlled by the various strata are somehow being significantly redistributed.

The absolute amounts involved in Moynihan's proposal are as important for appraising it as the relative shares involved. The full significance of payment levels cannot be confidently assessed because the answers to certain questions are not clear. Would the proposed child allowances be in addition to existing family welfare payments of various kinds? Or would the present payments be either wholly or partly reduced if the suggested federal plan were to go into effect? These questions remain open not only because the published proposal gives no answers to them; they are also difficult to answer because matters of eligibility and payment levels in current welfare programs are in the hands of the states, with widely differing results across the country. Regardless of how these imponderables might work out, however, Moynihan's schedule of allowances does not compare favorably with existing standards anywhere in the entire country—standards themselves widely regarded as a national scandal. Moynihan's proposal is $10 monthly for a child of average age. Compare this with presently existing average payments of Aid to Families with Dependent Children. The Moynihan proposal is less than one-third of the AFDC national average of $33.83. It amounts to less than one-quarter of the levels in a dozen states which range from over $40 to above $50. In fact, the proposed federal payment is comparable only to the present AFDC level in the state that stands at the bottom of the list of fifty—Mississippi's $9.13.

It would appear that, regardless of what state governments might do, there is one social segment that would receive needed new benefits under Moynihan's plan. According to reliable estimates, there are some fifteen million children of poor families in the United States, and only about three to four million of these are helped by AFDC. This means that upwards of ten million children in poverty receive no direct public aid in this country. These children would apparently be the principal and most urgently needy beneficiaries of the Moynihan proposal. Their benefit would, of course, be at the same level as that enjoyed by the publicly assisted poor in Mississippi. It works out to just over thirty cents per day for each child, allowing a few pennies less for infants and a few pennies more for adolescents. It is perhaps difficult to keep in simultaneous focus both the enormity of the problem these ten million children represent and the scale of this thirty-cent-a-day solution. Nevertheless, these figures do tend to support the position of local and national groups that have begun to organize since 1965 to demand a radical reorganization of the entire national public welfare system. The statistics may also help make clear why supporters of these demands might regard schemes like the Moynihan plan as disingenuous diversionary maneuvers rather than serious proposals.

Nor is it surprising that serious and sober observers have come to see Moynihan as both an intellectual apologist and a political strategist for maintaining the intergroup status quo in America, not only in race relations but with respect to the class system as well. This view is by no means limited to radical critics or civil rights partisans. For example, a thoughtful and moderate man, the eminent Negro American literary figure Ralph Ellison, has recently denounced not only Moynihan but also Nathan Glazer and others as "new apologists for segregation."

> Much hand-wringing was occasioned by Negro rejection of Moynihan's theory that the major source of Negro social difficulty is the Negro family. But it seems to me futile (and arrogant) to blame Negroes for rejecting a solution based on what they consider derogatory assumptions about themselves ... it was as though they were being told that their social salvation depended upon their accepting Mr. Moynihan's theory. Thus many Negroes felt that they were being bribed to accept a negative and damaging image of themselves which in terms of self-regard it was their triumph to have rejected. ... They also found it intriguing that ... the report ... was leaked to various reporters and conjured with in an effort to elect Mr. Moynihan to the New York City Council. So now, having refused further to burden their children with this money-baited psychological handicap, they are criticized for not being materialistic enough—while Pat Moynihan is regarded as a rejected savior who but for the wrong-headedness of Negro leaders ... could have brought about the social millennium.[17]

After dealing in similar terms with other writers, particularly Glazer, Ellison concludes:

> Our nation has thus far been fortunate in that anti-Negro racism has been relatively crude. ... It has not had the support of sophisticated post-Marxist, sociology-oriented apologetics. ... It would be tragically ironic if the violent anti-Negro racists were handed such ideological justification by intellectuals, who themselves could only reap chaos from supplying such a dangerous weapon. I believe, nevertheless, that such danger exists, and that it might well be being created in the form of just such apologetics. ...[18]

Since Ellison's criticism is couched in racial or ethnic terms, it does not state directly the meaning of Moynihan's position with respect to issues involving the interests of different social classes. Recently, however, Moynihan himself has made this quite clear. This clarification occurs in a speech some parts of which received nationwide publicity. In this statement Moynihan is addressing himself directly to a group of comfortable and affluent political liberals. Early in his address he reminds his audience that every one of them is "a person who has shared considerably in the rewards of American life, and who can look forward to continued sharing and, if anything, on more favorable terms." Having thus established the class interests of his hearers, he continues with a remarkable statement of what they would lose if the social system were changed.

> There are doubtless those among us so ungrateful, or so idealistic, as to wish or to be willing to give it all up in favor of a regime yet more generous in its distribution of worldly and psychic goods, but there is none of us, I repeat, who would not in fact have something considerable of both to lose in the exchange.[19]

Moynihan then goes on to contend that political forces which can be identified with liberalism have been in control of the national government during the last few years of growing political instability, preeminently the rise of public violence in American cities. From this argument he derives the central message of his address, to wit:

> that liberals [should] see more clearly their essential interest in the stability of the social order, and that given the present threats to that stability, it is necessary to seek out and make much more effective alliances with political conservatives who share that concern. . . .[20]

When the source of that instability is specified, it turns out to be a double threat, the first part being familiar and the second not surprising:

On the one hand the problems of the conditions of life and social behavior of the vast Negro underclass . . . a disorganized, angry, hurt group of persons easily given to self-destructive violence. And along with them another group of radical, nihilist youth, not themselves members of this underclass, but . . . determined to use it as an instrument of a violent apocalyptic confrontation. . . .[21]

Moynihan explicitly denies any hope of dialogue with the spokesmen for this threatening force and states without qualification that the only possible strategy is to separate that leadership from its mass following.

The point is a simple one: there is nothing whatever to be done to change the minds of the Negro nihilists, nor their white associates, that have been so much in evidence of late. Their course is set. The only option for the nation is to deprive them of the Negro underclass which is the source of their present strength.[22]

Following this, the reader searches in vain for a plausible suggestion as to how the liberal-conservative coalition should proceed to deny the "nihilists" their support. Moynihan forthrightly declares, "If the politics of stability are to come to anything, they must be translated into programs." Yet he offers nothing but two of the more shopworn conservative panaceas of recent years. In order that "state and local government" may "assume an effective role as an innovative and creative agent, it simply must begin to receive a share of Federal revenues on a permanent ongoing basis."[23] And "we must begin getting private business involved in domestic programs in a much more systematic, purposeful manner."[24] Thus does the "politics of stability" resolve itself into a strategy for strengthening existing centers of power and privilege, offered to the affluent so that they may preserve their advantages against a threat from the poor.

The Focal Concerns of a Middle-Class Scholar:
  Walter Miller

Most of the putative culture patterns ascribed to the lower-class poor by the writers reviewed here have a quality of hyperbole and simplification. One repeatedly finds that large, emotionally toned qualities are attributed to great masses of humanity that would be recognized in other contexts as quite heterogeneous: Negro Americans as a total category or the whole lower class of America. Here we shall consider two related tendencies, of which we saw earlier indications in the Frazier tradition, that are considerably more widespread. The first of these is a striking resemblance between learned, academic images of poverty culture and certain popular stereotypes of the poor that have great currency in the middle class. The second is a double tendency to view the poor as a threat to social stability and public order as these conditions are defined and valued by the non-poor, while projecting certain unresolved problems of the middle class onto the lower class.

Both these themes are well expressed in an influential article, "Lower Class Culture as a Generating Milieu of Gang Delinquency," by Walter Miller. This analysis purports to find the sources of delinquency and crime in half a dozen "focal concerns" put forward as distinctive of the lower class. Thus Miller tells us that lower-class people are concerned and anxious, and sometimes ambivalent about (1) trouble with the law versus law-abiding behavior; (2) toughness and masculinity versus weakness and effeminacy; (3) smartness or achievement by mental agility as opposed to gullibility or achievement through routine; (4) excitement and thrill as opposed to boredom and safety; (5) fate, fortune, or luck and their opposites; and (6) autonomy and freedom contrasted with dependency and constraint.

Evidently we are seriously being asked to believe that this series of "perceived alternatives" is nonexistent or has a totally different meaning outside the lower class. We are also being asked to agree that the threats of delinquency and crime in our society arise from the concern of the poor about these matters. The stereotyping and projection in this extraordinary thesis are obvious upon a moment's reflection. Where could one find a better brief inventory of unresolved value conflicts underlying the confusion and anomie of middle-class life in America than the many ambiguities and ambivalences associated with legality, masculinity, shrewdness, boredom, luck, and autonomy? As we college professors construct our theoretical models of poverty culture and our learned images of the poor, the least we can do is to ask ourselves whether these portrayals may not apply at least equally well to our students, colleagues, friends, and neighbors. Since we have a good deal more direct knowledge of these latter groups, this should be useful to the enterprise of determining how the poor differ from the rest of us. (For further examination of this formulation by Miller see chapter 5, pp. 135–38.)

Miller has also written on another matter of concern to some in the middle and upper strata of our society. This is the interesting problem of how to maintain a work force with minimal skills—people who will do the most menial jobs at the lowest rates of pay.

> How large a low-skilled laboring force does our society require? . . . From what sources are we to get the incumbents of these jobs, and where are they to receive the socialization and training needed to execute them? Under existing circumstances, the female-based child-rearing unit is a prime source of this essential pool of low-skilled laborers. It brings them into the world, and it furnishes them the values, the aspirations, and the psychic makeup that low-skill jobs require (e.g., high toleration of recurrent unemployment; high boredom tolerance; high flexibility with respect to work, residence, relational patterns; capacity to find life gratification outside the world of work).[25]

So it appears that the lower-class milieu generates something more than delinquency, indeed something that seems to be regarded as valuable by people who are not poor. The cause-and-effect relationships stated in these lines remain to be demonstrated. Nevertheless, it would be hard to find a statement that more starkly reflects the conflict between the interests of the poor and the interests of those who feel that their comfortable life depends on maintaining a "pool of low-skilled laborers." This passage is like much of the writing reviewed here: while demonstrating little about the cultural patterns of the poor it nevertheless implies a good deal about the values and perceived self-interest of the non-poor.

REPUTABILITY AND WORK IN THE WORLD OF
   DAVID MATZA

One recent exercise in learned and sophisticated stereotyping is outstanding chiefly for the large number of derogatory conceptions it brings together under the title "The Disreputable Poor." The author of this work takes pains to explain his title. "In the term disreputable I mean to introduce no personal judgment; but to reckon without the judgments made by other members of society, to ignore the stigma that adheres to this special kind of poverty, is to miss one of its key aspects."[26] This must rank as one of the best academic equivalents of the familiar sentiment: I don't have anything against them—it's just the way my neighbors feel. This is followed by a definition. "The disreputable poor are the people who remain unemployed, or casually or irregularly employed, even during periods approaching full employment and prosperity; for that reason, and others, they live in disrepute." The stratum in question is further described as a "persistent section of the poor who differ in a variety of ways from those who are deemed deserving . . . cannot be easily reformed or rehabilitated . . . are resistant and recalcitrant."[27] The definition is completed in the author's conclusion. "The disreputable poor are an immobilized segment of society located at a point in the social structure where poverty intersects with illicit pursuits. They are, in the evocative words of Charles Brace, 'the dangerous classes' who live in 'regions of squalid want and wicked woe.' "[28]

This is followed by a sizable catalog of value-laden terms ranging from the depressing Marxian label lumpenproletariat to Thorstein Veblen's colorful notion of a spurious leisure class. The idea that most appeals to Matza, however, is the nineteenth-century conception of the pauper, together with the derived distinction between poverty and pauperism. In this connection, he approvingly quotes a variety of more or less moralistic contentions that paupers have lost all self-respect and ambition, are not even ashamed of themselves, and just don't seem to care. These are the debased and de-classed types who deservedly languish at the bottom of the social hierarchy. Matza lists them off categorically: the drifters, drunks, beggars, tramps, criminals, and prostitutes. In Matza's scheme of the underclasses the most important group is one to which he gives a label that is uniquely expressive of middle-class scorn: the dregs. "The core of disreputable poverty consists of dregs—persons spawned in poverty and belonging to families who have been left behind by otherwise mobile ethnic populations."[29]

Within this context, Matza offers a familiar theory of pauperization. His exposition ranges over the history of poor laws in England, penal regulations and land tenure patterns associated with the Irish Famine, and the enslavement of Negroes in America. The key to pauperization in this view is "the association of work with a negative sanction," that is, a dissociation between labor and desired rewards. The contention is that the historical developments cited had the effect of inculcating boondoggling and indolence as well as other kinds of "demotivation." The stated result is that these disreputable tendencies became social traditions passed on from generation to generation. Thus again we find that what is really objectionable about the poor is that they allegedly do not share some of the most prized conventional values of the middle class. In this particular case, the essence of lower-class life is seen as a disreputable failure to manifest a virtue on which the middle class prides itself, and for which it praises the "stable working class": love of labor. Matza's historical interpretations clearly imply that masses of poor people were pauperized by the economic and political behavior of the non-poor. Yet he gives no hint that the privileged strata of today's society bear any responsibility for relieving the plight of the poor. On the contrary, his discussion leads one to infer that the only salvation for the victims of pauperization is for them to mobilize their own internal resources—resources which he himself has defined not even as nil but as a negative quantity. For example, he describes Negro Americans as the last important cohort of paupers in the United States. (This description is offered quite casually, without so much as a nod toward such well-known facts as the far worse statistics of deprivation for American Indians or the circumstance that the majority of our poor are white.) Matza concludes that a major reason why hard-core poverty persists in the United States is that the Negro population, that "other main carrier of the tradition of disreputable poverty in America, has only now begun to mobilize." Therefore the problem will remain until "the Negro mobilization has run its course."[30] So again we learn that whatever the ultimate historical causes, the principal operative source of poverty today is to be found among the poor themselves, and that somehow the remedy must come from the same source. In this instance, the logic of the argument seems to lead to the conclusion that the solution is a simple one: all the poor really need do is to learn the value of work. We are not told how this might have any effect upon poverty or inequality. It does seem clear, however, that this strategy might enable some people to graduate into the ranks of reputable poor. While this might not appeal very much to the potential graduates themselves, it obviously would please some others, including certain middle-class scholars. Perhaps this might even be another way to keep up the "pool of low-skilled laborers."

The International "Culture of Poverty,"
        with Implications for Social Science
        and Social Policy

The Anthropological Aims and Approaches of Oscar Lewis

For an anthropologist or anyone who appreciates the anthropological approach, turning to Oscar Lewis' writings on the "culture of poverty" after reviewing many sociological works on "lower-class culture" is likely to be a refreshing experience. Lewis is an anthropologist who knows what the theoretical concept of culture has meant in the works of his professional colleagues. He has employed ethnographic methods in much of his own research. It is clear that he shares many of the positive values associated with the idea of culture. Reading the published results of his field work with Mexicans and Puerto Ricans, where his notion of the "culture of poverty" is presented, one often feels that he came to know some of these people very well and achieved an empathetic rapport with them.

In his first extensive treatment of poverty Lewis tells us that this work grew out of the "conviction that anthropologists have a new function in the modern world: to serve as students and reporters of the great mass of peasants and urban dwellers of the underdeveloped countries who constitute almost 80% of the world's population."[1] At the same time he also makes clear his commitment to the essentials of the ethnographic approach. "To understand the culture of the poor it is necessary to live with them, to learn their language and customs, and to identify with their problems and aspirations. The anthropologist trained in the methods of direct observation and participation, is well prepared for this job, whether in his own or in a foreign country."[2] In his latest book Lewis has made his broader purposes quite explicit. "I have tried to give a voice to people who are rarely heard, and to provide the reader with an inside view of a style of life which is common in many of the deprived and marginal groups in our society . . . indeed, one of the major objectives of this volume is to bridge the gap in communication between the poor and the middle class personnel . . . lead to a more sympathetic view of the poor and their problems . . . provide a more rational basis for constructive social action."[3]

While Lewis' approach has thus grown directly out of traditional anthropological interests and concerns, he has also developed newer orientations that he felt were appropriate to his purposes. Early in this part of his career he observed that "peasant villages cannot be studied as isolates apart from the national culture; city dwellers cannot be studied as members of little communities. New approaches are necessary. . . ." The principal solution to these methodological problems adopted by Lewis was a technique of family study that has provided the main basis for all his work on the "culture of poverty," from *Five Families* to *La Vida*. In the Introduction to the first of these volumes he wrote, "Unlike earlier anthropological studies, the major focus of this study is the family rather than the community or the individual . . . whole family studies bridge the gap between the conceptual extremes of culture at one pole and the individual at the other; we need both culture and personality as they are interrelated in real life."[4] In the later volume the specific techniques involved are succinctly set forth.

> In summary, the major steps involved in producing a well-rounded family study are as follows: (1) census-type data are gathered on a large number of families selected on the basis of the major variables of interest to the study; (2) from this sample a smaller group of families are selected for more intensive study; (3) interviews are conducted with each family member to record their life story and to question them on a wide range

of topics; (4) a week or more of consecutive days are reconstructed on the basis of intensive interrogation; (5) complete days in the life of the family are observed and recorded; (6) recorded interviews are transcribed from the tapes; (7) typed data are translated, edited and organized; (8) reinterviewing is done to fill in gaps in the data; significant new data are translated and inserted; (9) the final version of the autobiographies and days are edited for publication.[5]

Additional techniques employed but not mentioned in this summary include the use of questionnaires, participant-observation, and clinical psychological testing. Matters covered in interviews and questionnaires included the collection of genealogies and the inventory of material possessions. Data resulting from some of these techniques, such as the psychological testing, have not been published as of late in 1967. The greater part of the information in the published works comes from the taped family biographies. The bulk of the books is made up of these edited verbatim transcripts, interspersed here and there with descriptions from observations of a day in the behavior of the family. Additional publications from the Puerto Rican research are expected.

INCONSISTENCIES BETWEEN ABSTRACTIONS AND DATA

A problem of both method and theory central to Lewis' work is a certain tension between the concept of culture, or culture patterns, and the conceptual units of the family or the individual. Writing retrospectively Lewis tells us, "It was my dissatisfaction with the high level of abstraction inherent in the concept of culture patterns which led me to turn away from anthropological community studies to the intensive study of families." He felt that this change of focus would enable him to get at "the very heart and soul of the phenomena we were concerned with, namely, the individual human being" and to avoid "overdrawn configurations that play up differences between cultures and tend to ignore the fundamental human similarities." Yet we find our author adding: "However, after having worked for a number of years on the level of family analysis I find it helpful to return again to the higher conceptual level of history and culture."[6] Thus does Lewis attempt to move back and forth from individual to family to culture. The attempt is not altogether successful. The transitions, connections, and interrelations among the different levels of analysis are never entirely clear. To my mind, this is a most important underlying difficulty in Lewis' approach, for it probably opens the way for additional weaknesses similar to those found in the sociological literature on "lower-class culture."

The organization of Lewis' books tends to highlight this difficulty. The pattern of these volumes begins with a brief introduction, ranging from fifteen pages in *Five Families* to forty-five pages in *La Vida*. Into these short sections are compressed generalized descriptions of the individual families, their community or neighborhood settings, the national history and social conditions of Mexico or Puerto Rico as the case may be, *and* the seventy-trait inventory of the "culture of poverty." Following these abbreviated but very broad introductions comes the relatively enormous bulk of highly particularistic and specific material from the daily lives or taped biographies of individual families, running in the case of *La Vida* to nearly 700 pages. This disjunction is most noticeable in the later works, where the author does not intervene in the bulk of the volume as either narrator or describer but simply presents a translated and edited form of his informants' words. This arrangement brings out the contrast between the interpretive descriptive passages by the author and the transcriptions of testimony from his informants. This makes the autobiographies seem almost like raw data, with all the problems of interpretation left to the reader.

This seeming invitation to interpret the evidence stimulates the critical reader to turn at intervals from the bulky transcribed texts back to the interpretive introductions. When the reader does this he finds some unanswered questions and some apparent contradictions. Among the unanswerable queries is one raised by more than one critical reviewer of Lewis' work: How representative are the autobiographies presented? In the Introduction to *La Vida*, the author briefly describes the Rios family, whose life stories take up most of the volume. He tells us that "the Rios family is not presented here as a typical Puerto Rican family but rather as representative of one style of life in a Puerto Rican slum. The frequency distribution of this style of life cannot be determined until we have many comparable studies from other slums in Puerto Rico and elsewhere." This is refreshing methodological candor. However, it leaves us unable to evaluate the validity of a crucial statement appearing in the same paragraph: "The Rios family, their friends and neighbors, reflect many of the characteristics of the subculture of poverty, characteristics which are widespread in Puerto Rico but which are by no means exclusively Puerto Rican."[7]

If the wider occurrence, in actuality, of the behaviors and beliefs described by members of the Rios family is not known, what is the basis for presenting them as representatives of a "subculture of poverty"? What chain of evidence or body of empirical data links the concrete phenomena, ascribed to the Rios family by their own testimony, to a way of life shared by the poor or some large part of the poor in Puerto Rico and elsewhere? While Lewis does not answer these questions explicitly, it would seem from his methodological presentation that the most likely sources of such evidence are what he calls "census-type data," plus the help of social workers in locating sample families. These are, of course, precisely the kinds of sources we found to be so inadequate and suspect in the work of others focused on the notion of "lower-class culture."

In some respects it appears that the Rios family are not representative but, rather, manifest minority patterns, even within their particular slum community. Any reader of *La Vida* will remember how important prostitution is in the lives of all the Rios women. Lewis tells us in his Introduction that only one third of the families in this slum had any history of prostitution, and he adds that "prostitution has certainly made a difference in the Rios family." Among the special features specified as resulting from the importance of prostitution in this family history are differences in income and spending patterns, childhood exposure to sex and neglect of children, a reinforced negative self-image, and a selective factor influencing the type of men who married Rios women. In this connection Lewis says, "It seems to me that the history of prostitution has not caused any major changes in the basic patterns of their family life. This conclusion is based on a comparison of their lives before and after they became prostitutes."[8] While this may be a valid interpretation from the life histories of the Rios women, it cannot be assumed that it would hold for comparisons between this family and other domestic groups in the same slum, elsewhere in the Puerto Rican lower class, or more widely in the "culture of poverty."

Beyond this, there are some indications that the subjects of *La Vida* were chosen, not because of their representativeness, but on the contrary because they manifested deviant extremes. Note, for example, Lewis' statement that "the Rios family is closer to the expression of an unbridled id than any other people I have studied."[9] Especially coming from a student of the "culture of poverty" who has written so much about uncontrolled rage, violence, and sexuality, this would seem to be a singular statement of uniqueness and hardly a description of representativeness. Nevertheless, we find our author easily identifying the apparently deviant behavior of this family with a putative culture pattern. "The remarkable stability in some of the behavior patterns of the Rios family over four generations, which span a period of rapid change in Puerto Rican society, suggests that we are dealing with a tenacious culture pattern. This can be seen clearly in the high incidence of early marriages, of free unions, of multiple

spouses and of illegitimate children." Following closely
upon these lines comes another illuminating but contradictory
passage. "The history of the Rios family . . . suggests that
the pattern of free unions and multiple spouses is not limited
to the poor. It has been a widespread pattern among wealthy
rural families; Fernanda's great-grandfather, a well-to-do
landowner, is a case in point. This illustrates a general
proposition . . . namely, the remarkable similarities between
some aspects of the lives of the very poor and the very rich."[10]

Thus in the space of four or five pages we have the charac-
ters of *La Vida* presented, in turn, as (1) typical of the culture
of the poor, (2) following a life style of unknown frequency
and distribution, (3) deeply affected by a specialized occupational pattern confined to one third of their community, (4)
characterized by an extreme deviance unique in their chroni-
cler's experience, and (5) spanning the gap between the upper
and lower classes both in wealth and in family patterns. There
can be little wonder then that a curious but careful reader experiences difficulty in placing these life stories clearly in a
wider context. These difficulties merely illustrate the broader
problem of discerning clear relationships between these case
histories on the one hand and the abstraction of the "culture
of poverty" on the other.

When one compares the abstract conception of poverty
culture with concrete descriptions of the local community,
what appear to be straightforward contradictions immediately arise. Consider first the following generalized statement:

> When we look at the culture of poverty on the local com-
> munity level, we find . . . above all a minimum of organization
> beyond the level of the nuclear and extended family. Occasion-
> ally there are informal, temporary groupings . . . the existence
> of neighborhood gangs . . . represents a considerable advance
> beyond the zero point of the continuum that I have in mind.
> Indeed, it is the low level of organization which gives the culture
> of poverty its marginal and anachronistic quality . . . most
> primitive peoples have achieved a higher level of socio-cultural
> organization than our modern urban slum dwellers.[11]

Then compare this description from a few pages earlier in the same work.

> The setting for the story of the Rios family is La Esmeralda, an old and colorful slum in San Juan, built on a steep embankment between the city's ancient fort walls and the sea. Squeezed into an area not more than five city blocks long and a few hundred yards wide are 900 houses inhabited by 3,600 people. . . .
>
> Seen from the wall above the slum looks almost prosperous. This is because all the houses have roofs of new green tar paper, a contribution from the mayoress, *doña* Felica Rinzon. . . .
>
> Within the larger settlement are three subdivisions, . . . these subdivisions are connected with San Juan by four entrances. . . .
>
> Even though La Esmeralda is only ten minutes away from the Governor's Palace and the heart of San Juan, it is physically and socially marginal to the city. The wall above it stands as a kind of symbol separating it from the city. La Esmeralda forms a little community of its own with a cemetery, a church, a small dispensary and maternity clinic, and one elementary school. There are many small stores, bars and taverns. . . .
>
> To the people of Greater San Juan, La Esmeralda has a bad reputation . . . yet conditions are said to have been much worse twenty years ago. . . . Today the residents of La Esmeralda think of it as a relatively elegant, healthful place, with its beautiful view of the sea, its paved streets, its new roofs, the absence of mosquitoes, the low rentals and its nearness to their places of work.[12]

These two passages simply cannot be reconciled in terms that are consistent with the intended meaning of Lewis' work. Taken at face value, the description of La Esmeralda as "a little community of its own" can only mean that this slum is not part of the "culture of poverty" defined as lacking virtually all community organization. While this interpretation is clearly at odds with Lewis' intended message, it is difficult to draw any other conclusion from the material he presents. Thus again the reader is left to wonder about the empirical foundations for the concept of a "culture of poverty." In this connection it might also be noted that other investigators have found well-defined community structures among the urban poor. An example that is notable because it contradicts common expectations is William Mangin's recent finding that shantytown squatter settlements around Latin American cities manifest a high degree of adaptive community organization. (For further attention to community patterns among the urban poor see the Appendix, pp. 173–77.)

When we turn to the lengthy autobiographies and brief descriptions of daily behavior making up the bulk of these volumes, we are confronted with a hugh mass of unanalyzed and unevaluated material. It is most difficult to determine the validity of this material, its reliability, and even its precise relevance to Lewis' theoretical formulations. The author suggests that the autobiographies present a subjective picture of life among the poor, while the descriptions of daily behavior constitute a more objective portrayal. He also suggests that the appearance of the same events in life stories told by several different persons makes it possible to check the reliability of one informant against another. Whatever utility these suggestions may have, their application is left entirely to the reader, for the author has added virtually no commentary to these texts. Where there are internal contradictions, the reader has no basis for preferring one source over another, save whatever impressions he may have gained from the texts themselves.

Oscar Lewis' books tell the reader more about his methods of field research than do the writings of many anthropologists. Within the context of this refreshing and welcome candor, it is all the more frustrating that important questions remain unanswered about how Lewis obtained his taped autobiographies. His fullest account of this process appears in one of the earlier works, *The Children of Sanchez*. Here we learn of Lewis' feeling that he achieved a warm personal relationship with his informants and that it was essentially their feeling of friendship that led them to recount their life stories. The clear implication is that this circumstance enhances the reliability of the informants' testimony, an implication that this reviewer for one is inclined to accept at face value on the basis of his own ethnographic experience. Nevertheless, one's confidence would be increased considerably if the problem of rapport and its effects on informant testimony were discussed critically, with the inclusion of at least a few concrete examples. Lewis also tells us that most of his taping was done in the privacy of his office or his home, which were apparently far from the accustomed milieu of his informants. Again there is no critical discussion of the possible influence of these circumstances.

Lewis tells us that during some parts of the interviews he employed "a directive approach" in order to get his informants to cover systematically a broad range of subject matter which he hoped would add up to "their total view of the world." He expresses his belief that many of his questions stimulated informants to deal with matters they might otherwise never have thought about or volunteered to talk about. In addition to direct questioning he encouraged free association, and he adds that he made an attempt to be a good listener. All this is certainly helpful and indeed goes beyond the standards achieved by many anthropological reporters. Nevertheless, it seems to me that it would have been easy to go just a little farther and give the reader a really clear impression of just how the autobiographical material was elicited. A few sample questions, perhaps designed as examples of different interview techniques, and a few lines to illustrate materials forthcoming from both directive and nondirective approaches would surely have gone a long way toward answering our queries.

For this reader at any rate, these presently unanswered questions about method assume even greater importance when one considers another issue: the nature and extent of editorial influences on the shape and content of the autobiographies in their final published form. In this connection, an explanatory paragraph by Lewis deserves full quotation.

> In preparing these interviews for publication, I have eliminated my questions and have selected, arranged, and organized their materials into coherent life stories. If one agrees with Henry James that life is all inclusion and confusion while art is all discrimination and selection, then these life histories have something of both art and life. I believe this in no way reduces the authenticity of the data or their usefulness for science. For those of my colleagues who are interested in the raw materials, I have the taped interviews available.[13]

This is followed by indications that the amount and kind of editing imposed varied from one informant to another. It is made clear, however, that the author often reorganized the material, selecting some portions of the testimony and eliminating others. Without more explicit specification of editing criteria, it is difficult to estimate where these autobiographies stand on the continuum stretching from raw data, through evidence merely organized for convenience, to an intellectual creation fashioned by the editor from informant testimony.

Unlike lesser scholars, Oscar Lewis does not shrink from admitting that "my training as an anthropologist, my years of familiarity with Mexican culture, my own values, and my personality influenced the final outcome of this study."[14] He does fail, however, to provide us with sufficient information to serve as a basis for estimating *how* these influences affected the shape of his published material. This problem is serious because of the very way in which the material is presented, with no overt indications of where the author-editor has intervened in the hundreds and hundreds of pages that make up the life stories. When the authorship of narrative or descriptive writing is clearly assignable to a single source, the reader is at least able to develop from internal evidence reasonable hypotheses about viewpoints and biases being expressed. In the present cases, however, the organization, emphases, and selective choices that produced the final works come in unknown proportions from two different sources with different viewpoints. It is therefore difficult or impossible for the reader to apply the usual criteria of internal evidence in making judgments of biases or other sources of distortion in operation. This in turn leaves the reader at sea in evaluating both consistencies and inconsistencies between the autobiographies, on the one hand, and Lewis' descriptive and analytical passages, on the other.

To explore some of the relationships between the "culture of poverty," as described in the abstract, and the evidence to be found in the autobiographies, let us return to Lewis' latest major work, *La Vida*. Of the many aspects of life which might be dealt with here, it is not possible to cover more than one without unduly extending the discussion. The area I have chosen for this purpose is what might be called orientation toward the wider world, as manifested by expressions of interest in politics, class consciousness, ethnic identity, and national identification. In Lewis' account of those who live by the "culture of poverty" he pictures them as removed and alienated, ignorant and uninterested, uninvolved and apathetic toward all these dimensions of the wider world. In his words, "The lack of effective participation and integration in the major institutions of the larger society is one of the crucial characteristics of the culture of poverty. This is a complex matter and results from a variety of factors which may include . . . fear, suspicion, or apathy. . . . People with a culture of poverty . . . usually do not belong to labor unions, are not members of political parties. . . ."[15] The principal integrative role for group consciousness that Lewis allows is a purely local one. This is indicated by his statement that "when the population constitutes a distinct ethnic, racial or language group . . . then the sense of local community approaches that of a village community."[16] (Lewis notes that Africans in the Republic of South Africa and Negroes in the United States may be exceptions to this generalization.) In conclusion Lewis generalizes as follows. "People with a culture of poverty are provincial and locally oriented . . . they know only their own troubles, their local conditions, their own neighborhood . . . usually they do not have the knowledge, the vision or the ideology to see the similarities between their problems and those of their counterparts elsewhere . . . they are not class-conscious. . . ."[17]

Now the autobiographies of the Rios women and their consorts and kinsmen certainly do contain a great many expressions of personal, local, and other narrowly defined interests. It seems fair to suggest that this is just what we should expect from ordinary people anywhere, perhaps especially when their life stories are being elicited by a social scientist explicitly interested in family studies. What is surprising in view of Lewis' abstract description, however, is the quite substantial expressions of wider interests by these same informants.

Consider the following random sampling of such expressions by six of these informants, three women and three men. Fernanda, the *grande dame* of the Rios family, repeatedly generalizes intelligently about the life and social position of prostitutes. One such disquisition culminates in a pithy dissertation on the relationship between whores, the police, and the system of justice. Subsequently she describes the passionately argumentative allegiance given by another character to the Popular Party, and she then goes on to explain why she and all her offspring have always been Statehood Republicans. Erasmo, who lived with Fernanda for seven years, is allotted only fourteen pages for his account of those years. Within this space, he spends some two and a half pages comparing socioeconomic opportunities within Puerto Rico and the United States, touches lightly on the politics of four other Latin American countries, and expounds on the major political issues, parties, and personalities in Puerto Rico.

Fernanda's eldest daughter Soledad gives a class-consciously approving description of her husband Octavio's career of robbing the rich and sharing with the poor. She draws the moral that there is no justice against the wealthy from the fact that Octavio was shot to death by one of his intended victims, a wealthy proprietor who received no penalty for the shooting. At one point Soledad describes her unavailing efforts, first to find employment, then to obtain increased aid from the welfare establishment; she relates these experiences systematically, albeit somewhat cynically, to the nature of Puerto Rican politics. Here and there Soledad offers rather extensive reflections on race relations in the United States and the implications with respect to education and employment for Puerto Ricans and other groups. While living in New York, Soledad even made a pilgrimage to Washington to attend the funeral of President Kennedy. In describing this as a very moving experience, she explains her feelings toward Kennedy in terms of his administration's policies and programs on race relations and aid to Puerto Rico. In addition she compares her feelings about Kennedy with her evaluation of Muñoz Marin, Eisenhower, Roosevelt, and Johnson. Soledad's autobiography ends with an earthy and passionate assertion of Puerto Rican national identity. "I want to be buried in Puerto Rico because that's my country. Even if I do live in New York, I never forget my country. I wouldn't change it for the world. That's where I was born and that's where I want to be buried . . . but not here. Shit! I don't care what happens here, I'm only interested in what goes on in my own country, in what happens to Puerto Ricans who belong to my race. Nobody else matters to me."[18]

The testimony of Benedicto, Soledad's husband at the time the autobiographies were taped, fills only a few pages. Benedicto delivers himself of a number of generalizations and comparisons about the cultures of the United States and Puerto Rico. He also explains in considerable detail the benefits that he feels he and others receive from membership and active participation in the National Maritime Union. Another of Fernanda's daughters, Felicita, has a good deal to say about the ambiguities and ambivalences of Puerto Rican and American national identification. Elsewhere Felicita produces what is in effect an informal political essay. This passage includes descriptions of attendance by several members of the Rios family at a political rally, and visits by national figures to La Esmeralda; her own commentary on the political process and personalities within the slum community; and remarks about the relationship of all this to the wider political scene both in Puerto Rico and in the United States.

Simplicio is Fernanda's son, living in New York and working in a clothing factory owned by a Jewish entrepreneur. Within this context, Simplicio expounds at some length on the nature of the Jews as a people, their history, their culture, and their relations with other ethnic groups. Like the other informants, Simplicio has much to say in broad terms about the interrelated problems of Puerto Rican status in the United States, American race relations, Puerto Rican party politics, and social reform in Puerto Rico. Finally, Simplicio presents an organized discussion of the domestic politics of the United States in relation to international affairs, including Cuba, Castro, and Communism. Toward the end of this discussion, Simplicio mentions that he has just reached the age of twenty-one and wishes to vote in the next election. He adds that he has been unable, in spite of some effort, to discover how or where to register as a voter.

This last detail from Simplicio's story is an appropriate point from which to turn back again to the generalized picture of the "culture of poverty." This detail reminds us that Lewis stresses lack of actual participation in the wider world. He treats participation as distinct from, and not less important than, lack of awareness or interest in wider affairs. It is quite clear that even such portions of the autobiographies as those just cited contain much verbal expression of interest and knowledge, with relatively little evidence of actual behavior outside the circle of household and kinsmen. It seems fair to suggest, however, that this should not be altogether unexpected when the attention of the interviewer-editor, and thus presumably of the informants as well, is so focused on family life. Moreover, failures in participation such as Simplicio's unsuccessful attempt to translate his political orientation into action do not appear to stem from lack of motivation or intention. They seem to be due to other factors, including some that are not only external to the individual but also outside the life of the poor altogether. For example, there can be little doubt that if those who control the political organizations of New York attached great importance to participation by the Simplicios of the city they could find them and register them as voters. We shall return in later pages to this problem of external versus internal causes of behavior among the poor.

INCONGRUITY BETWEEN INFORMATIONAL FOCUS AND THEORETICAL VISTA

One important point emerges thus far. The partial inventory of broad extra-family and supra-local interests and concerns cited from the Rios histories above simply cannot be reconciled with Lewis' portrayal of the poor as well nigh totally isolated and confined to a narrow little world of personal events and family affairs. Such contradictions between concrete evidence and theoretical model are a most important part of Lewis' failure to clarify the connections between his main levels of analysis: the individual, the family, the residential locale or community, the cultural pattern ascribed to the lower class, and such larger sociocultural units as the nation. This difficulty stems ultimately, I believe, from Lewis' intellectual ambivalence toward the culture concept itself and his resulting methodological orientation. In short, Lewis has become so committed to his focus on the family as the unit of study that his approach does not provide adequate evidence of life beyond the confines of the household.

This apparent limitation may be created in part at least by Lewis' selection of research materials for publication. His descriptions of his field methods make it appear that he may have evidence of many other aspects of life which are not directly represented in his published works on the "culture of poverty." This obviously leaves open the possibility that future publications will remedy the difficulties and weaknesses cited here. In examining the work as it stands, however, we must evaluate it on the basis of what is available to the reading public.

Judged from this viewpoint, it must be said that none of the various works focused on poverty culture show, either in manifest method or in reported data, the fully rounded ethnographic approach employed by Lewis in earlier research, such as his descriptions of the Mexican village Tepoztlan. In these earlier studies, as in most ethnographic accounts, family life is only one among many equally important aspects of social existence: the economic system, the wider social structure, the political order from village to nation, the individual life cycle, and ritual and ideology. This holistic portrayal of a way of life is clearly based on methods involving inquiry and observation focused on an integral complex including most major aspects of existence, and dealing with all the major levels of social integration. In other words, both method and data are geared to discovering and presenting the culture in its entirety, "that complex whole . . . acquired by man as a member of society."

In the poverty-culture studies, on the contrary, the focus is so restricted to the family that the social system as a whole and its culture patterns become little more than a shadowy backdrop for personal and household intimacies. There is no doubt that this orientation is perfectly legitimate for some kinds of research. What this approach cannot adequately support, however, is the portrayal of a culture, a whole way of life. If Lewis presented these works as studies of family life among the poor, there would be no quarrel of this sort with his method or his selection of evidence. He could then quite properly leave the broader problem of the whole culture of the poor to other research workers, or perhaps to later works of his own. The serious weakness of these studies as they stand is that, in them, Lewis has insisted on returning to the cultural level of portrayal and analysis without presenting evidence adequately supporting his abstract model at this level. The wider importance of this weakness stems from the fact that this very notion of a *culture* of poverty has so greatly influenced public knowledge, attitudes, and policies.

One searches in vain through these books for an integrated portrayal of the whole way of life constructed from factual data that span the main dimensions of social existence. *La Vida*, for instance, is full of hints and seeming indications which arouse a curiosity in the reader that is never satisfied. The cultural context within which the Rios family lives out its lives never becomes clear. We find no more than the sketchiest statistical summary to represent the economic behavior of the slum dwellers as a group. We learn almost nothing of the economic institutions, local or otherwise, that impinge upon their lives. Apart from the few Rios households, kinship and social organization receive no more than conventional summary demographic treatment. Tantalizing bits and pieces emerge as seeming indicators of the life of La Esmeralda as a community. Yet we never learn how this community is structured, and we gain no more than disconnected indications of the social processes that go on within it. Political patterns and problems are especially intriguing because of the many references to them in the autobiographies, but without any other reference points it is impossible even to understand fully the Rios' political reactions, much less to obtain a clear picture of the political context in which they live. Similarly, our curiosity is repeatedly piqued by references to Roman Catholicism and spiritism, but we never discover the institutional or ideological forms that shape people's lives in these areas. There are, as we have seen, many unanalyzed data from specific individuals on socioeconomic values, individual and group identity, secular knowledge and world view. Yet we find no integrated portrayal of these and related phenomena for any group, except for the unconvincing and contradictory abstract model of the "culture of poverty."

What we end up with is a series of overlapping family portraits or self-portraits presented in isolation from their natural or actual context. Introducing these portrayals with a highly abstract model of the context—a model we must also suspect to be somewhat artificial—only *seems* to resolve this difficulty. As we have seen, careful comparison of the concrete life histories with the introductory abstractions only raises more unanswered questions. Despite their value in other respects, these works do not succeed in what has generally been regarded as their principal contribution: they do not present a convincing case for the existence of an identifiable culture.

Another contrast between Lewis' earlier and later findings has to do with the question of social disorganization or cultural disintegration. Some years ago Lewis studied former villagers from Tepoztlan who had gone to live in Mexico City. This work was an outgrowth of his ethnographic research on the village community. Its immediate frame of reference therefore was the integrated village culture. It should also be noted that many of the families and individuals with whom Lewis worked in the city were very poor and lived in poverty-stricken *vecindades* quite similar to the settings of Lewis' later and better known family studies. The principal finding in the report of the earlier urban research is succinctly conveyed by its title: "Urbanization Without Breakdown."

Selected summary descriptions give substance to this interpretation.

> There is little evidence of disorganization and breakdown. . . . Family life remains strong. . . . Family cohesiveness and extended family ties increase in the city, fewer cases of separation and divorce occur, no cases of abandoned mothers and children, no cases of persons living alone or of unrelated families living together. Household composition is similar to village patterns . . . Religious life in the city becomes more Catholic

and disciplined. . . . The system of *compadrazgo* has undergone important changes but remains strong. . . . Village ties remain strong, with much visiting back and forth. [19]

Thus the picture of life that emerges when people's behavior is seen in the context of a fully rounded cultural system appears to be quite different from the impressions fostered by projecting family histories against a schematic backdrop that highlights alleged disorganization. At the very least, this description of urban patterns including slum life stands as a striking exception to the general model of the "culture of poverty." (For further analysis of this model see chapter 5, pp. 129–35.)

PATHOLOGY, POLITICS, POLICIES, AND PROGRAMS

Were it not for this ill-conceived creation of the general concept of poverty culture—with its appeal to popular imagination and public attention—the work of Oscar Lewis probably would not have so strongly affected community attitudes and public policies. It should perhaps be made explicit here, before going on with this aspect of our discussion, that Lewis' writings indicate his conscious and definite intention that humane and progressive results should flow from his work in the areas of public understanding and community programs. Much of the public impact of the "culture of poverty" idea has of course been mediated by other channels including many secondary sources, specialized applications or misapplications, and popularized discussions. Obviously such applications as using the poverty-culture concept to justify restricted educational opportunities must be understood and dealt with separately from the original work. Indeed, because of Lewis' obviously constructive and humanitarian intentions, it is tempting to absolve him of any responsibility for its assimilation to the pernicious popular and scholarly tradition of "lower-class culture" and the policy correlates of this tradition. This temptation will be resisted here, in order to explore the question whether certain elements inherent in the poverty culture concept may lend themselves to these unfortunate applications.

We have seen that in the social science literature there is a considerable emphasis on a heavily negative approach to the behaviors and values that are thought to be distinctive of the lower class or the poor. Scarcely a description can be found that does not dwell on the noxiousness, pathology, distortion, disorganization, instability, or incompleteness of poverty culture as compared with life of the middle classes. Lewis has taken some pains to dissociate himself from this orientation, in its more simplistic forms at least. Discussing his view of the "culture of poverty", he writes as follows: "This view directs attention to the fact that the culture of poverty in modern nations is not only a matter of economic deprivation, of disorganization or of the absence of something. It is also something positive and provides some rewards without which the poor could hardly carry on." "That is, the core of culture is its positive adaptive function. I, too, have called attention to some of the adaptive mechanisms in the culture of poverty. . . ."[20] In spite of all this, however, Lewis' description of poverty culture runs very heavily to such negative traits as "lack of effective participation," "minimum of organization," "absence of childhood," "high incidence of the abandonment of wives and children," and "a high incidence of maternal deprivation, of orality, of weak ego structure, confusion of sexual identification, a lack of impulse control . . . little ability to defer gratification and to plan for the future . . . and a high tolerance for psychological pathology of all sorts."[21] This is, of course, much the same list of disabilities found in standard sociological descriptions of "lower-class culture."

There is a similar pattern in the position taken by Lewis on the problem of psychosocial pathology among the poor. First he says that "psychiatrists, clinical psychologists and social workers who have read the autobiographies and psychological tests of the people I have studied, have often found more negative elements and pathology than I am willing to grant." While he feels that the Rios family, for example, does have "a history of psychopathology" and that they "would probably be classified as a multi-problem family by most social workers," nevertheless he stresses what he calls "the strengths in this family": "fortitude, vitality, resilience, and ability to cope," "their own sense of dignity and morality . . . kindness, generosity. . . ."[22] A little farther on in the same discussion, however, Lewis formulates the generalization that has most often and most widely been seized upon in general discussions of the "culture of poverty": "Once it comes into existence it tends to perpetuate itself from generation to generation because of its effect on children. By the time slum children are age six or seven, they have usually absorbed the basic values and attitudes of their subculture and are not psychologically geared to take full advantage of changing conditions or increased opportunities which may occur in their lifetime."[23] This proposition, more than any other, has been enlarged and reemphasized over and over again by many other writers; it has been used to justify all kinds of antipoverty programs designed to inculcate middle-class virtues into the children of the poor; and it has been widely employed to build a bridge across whatever gap exists between the concept of poverty culture and the notion of a disabling way of life peculiar to the lower class.

Lewis makes it clear that he is well aware of a longstanding ideological conflict between "two opposite evaluations of the nature of the poor." He refers to one view of the poor as "blessed, virtuous, upright, serene, independent, honest, kind and happy," as opposed to the other vision of them as "evil, mean, violent, sordid, and criminal." Lewis is also aware that this conflict is "reflected in the in-fighting that is going on in the current war against poverty" between those who "stress the great potential of the poor for self-help, leadership and community organization" and those who "point to the sometimes irreversible, destructive effect of poverty upon individual character, and therefore emphasize the need for guidance and control to remain in the hands of the middle class, which presumably has better mental health."[24] Lewis does not present anything that could be called a straightforward resolution of this issue. I believe it is fair to say that he tries to explore and clarify the issue rather than to resolve it. The net result seems to be that, by implication at least, some validity is granted to each of the contradictory positions. It may be that this merely means it is easy for either side to find support within the writings of this author. Perhaps the "culture of poverty" is most often used to buttress the emphasis upon internal disabilities within the lower class mainly because this position is in the ascendancy generally for other reasons. Nevertheless, it is certainly true that those who hold this position can find much support in Lewis' books that develop the notion of a poverty culture. The main point to be emphasized here is a somewhat different one. If it is true, as I have argued earlier, that the existence of a "culture of poverty" has not been convincingly demonstrated, then the concept does not constitute a valid support for either side of the ideological controversy. This is what makes it most unfortunate that the poverty-culture idea should be so influential in public policy as a factor supporting bias in one ideological direction.

Another element of Lewis' thought, which is also relevant to policy problems and ideological issues, makes it appear more certain that psychological and social disorganization are inherent qualities in his conception of poverty culture. This is the distinction Lewis makes between poverty as such and a culture of poverty. He uses this contrast in describing groups of people who, in his view, do not live by a culture of poverty in spite of being poverty-stricken. When one considers his examples, it becomes clear that what distinguishes these groups is their personal and social integration even under conditions of poverty. Three kinds of traditional cultural systems are put forward as satisfying these criteria in spite of dire material deprivation: nonliterate primitive peoples, the lower castes of India, and the Jews of Eastern Europe. The argument becomes more complex when Lewis adds to this list Cuba since the Castro revolution, together with the clear implication that previously many Cubans did live by a "culture of poverty." Generalizing tentatively, he remarks that he is "inclined to believe that the culture of poverty does not exist in the socialist countries." To this is added the opinion that "there is relatively little of what I would call the culture of poverty" in the United States, even among ethnic minorities, "because of the advanced technology, high level of literacy, the development of mass media and the relatively high aspiration of all sectors of the population." Among Negro Americans in particular, Lewis feels that the civil rights movement has done much to overcome the poverty culture. He summarizes:

> In effect, we find that in primitive societies and in caste societies, the culture of poverty does not develop. In socialist, fascist and in highly developed capitalist societies with a welfare state the culture of poverty tends to decline. I suspect that the culture of poverty flourishes in, and is generic to, the early free enterprise stage of capitalism and that it is also endemic in colonialism.[25]

Exploring these ideas further, Lewis seems to suggest that the essentials for converting a "culture of poverty" into something else are organization, solidarity, and hope—apparently almost any kind of organization, used in service of any cause, and hope enlivened by any vision. This thesis is both stated in the abstract and put forth to explain concrete cases. The general formulation is as follows.

> When the poor become class conscious or active members of trade union organizations, or when they adopt an internationalist outlook on the world, they are no longer part of the culture of poverty although they may still be desperately poor. Any movement, be it religious, pacifist, or revolutionary, which organizes and gives hope to the poor and effectively promotes

solidarity and a sense of identification with larger groups, destroys the psychological and social core of the culture of poverty.[26]

The main specific case is post-revolutionary Cuba, where Lewis recently revisited the same slum community and some of the same families he had studied in pre-Castro days.

> The physical aspect of the slum had changed very little, except for a beautiful new nursery school. It was clear that the people were still desperately poor, but I found much less of the despair, apathy and hopelessness which are so diagnostic of urban slums in the culture of poverty. They expressed great confidence in their leaders and hope for a better life in the future. The slum itself was now highly organized, with block committees, educational committees, party committees. The people had a new sense of power and importance. They were armed and were given a doctrine which glorified the lower class as the hope of humanity.[27]

As a theory of culture change, these formulations are not impressive. The central idea, that human groups with unsatisfying ways of life can be reinvigorated by enthusiastic involvement in a social movement promising a new culture, is a respectable conception with a long history. This idea has been at the core of other recent theoretical models in anthropology and other fields. Among these models have been some that explain more than Lewis' propositions and do so without recourse to the doubtful notion of a "culture of poverty." It should also be noted here that Lewis makes no attempt to present these propositions as grand theory and makes no great claims for them.

He does note that his views on these matters have a certain relevance to recent discussions stressing a conflict between the Marxian position that the lumpenproletariat is antirevolutionary or reactionary, and Frantz Fanon's argument that the same stratum has great revolutionary potential. Lewis appears to identify the lumpenproletariat with those who live by a "culture of poverty." Again as on earlier issues, however, he takes a kind of middle ground rather than adopting either side in the controversy as his own. The poor, he indicates, may or may not be a source of revolution, depending on "the national context and the particular historical circumstances."[28]

Again, it would seem that there is something here that might be used to support almost any ideological orientation (even fascism is mentioned as a movement which overcomes the "culture of poverty"). It may be argued that there can be no objection to this on purely scholarly or scientific grounds, but the same argument can hardly be made when policy questions are involved. From this viewpoint, it is most disappointing to find that in the end Lewis chooses to lay all his emphasis *not* on eliminating poverty but rather on doing away with the "*culture* of poverty." This position seems quite extraordinary, when we realize that Lewis also believes that poverty itself can be more easily and readily wiped out than the "culture" he associates with it.

On the latter point Lewis is quite explicit: "It is much more difficult to eliminate the culture of poverty than to eliminate poverty *per se*"; and again, "The elimination of physical poverty *per se* may not be enough to eliminate the culture of poverty."[29] Only at the very close of his essay on poverty culture does he permit himself to write explicitly of "solutions" for "the future." Even here he does not allow himself to recommend anything straightforwardly, but in fact merely describes in a very few lines the "solutions," as he sees them, that are presently being carried out. By coupling these short descriptions with the reference to the future he manages to convey the impression, perhaps inadvertently, that he does not think there are any alternatives to these "solutions." In any case, he mentions no other possibilities. For these final generalizations, he devotes one short paragraph to the United States and one to the underdeveloped nations, basing his classification on the contention that poverty culture affects

much of the population in the latter, but only a minority of
the American populace.

> In the United States, the major solution proposed by planners
> and social workers in dealing with multi-problem families and
> the so-called hard core of poverty has been to attempt slowly
> to raise their level of living and to incorporate them into the
> middle class. Wherever possible, there has been some reliance
> upon psychiatric treatment.
>
> In the underdeveloped countries, however . . . a social-work
> solution does not seem feasible. Because of the magnitude of
> the problem, psychiatrists can hardly begin to cope with it . . .
> revolutions frequently succeed in abolishing some of the basic
> characteristics of the culture of poverty even when they do not
> succeed in abolishing poverty itself.[30]

It is perhaps possible that these lines were intended to carry
a subtly ironic implication that current measures to alleviate
the plight of the poor leave something to be desired. If so, it
seems certain that the message is sufficiently cryptic to escape
the notice of the average reader among either the lay public
or the ranks of policymakers and social service personnel.

The only other interpretation of these lines that appears
meaningful is that Oscar Lewis really believes in an absolute
priority of the "culture of poverty" over poverty itself. Ultimately, he is saying that the alleged culture patterns of the
lower class are more important in their lives than the condition of being poor and, consistently, that it is more important
for the power holders of society to abolish these lifeways than
to do away with poverty—even if eradicating poverty can be
done more quickly and easily.

What can be the basis for this set of judgments and valua-
tions? It is difficult to imagine what this might be, except a
profound implicit conviction that the lifeways of the poor are
inherently deserving of destruction. If it is relatively easy to do
away with poverty itself, then why not do so and then let the
ex-poor live as they please? Or if we believe there is a "culture of poverty" which is not good for those who live by it,
then why not first tackle the more tractable problem of

relieving their material deprivation and then go on to build upon their more comfortable circumstances in order to save them from those more difficult and deep-seated culture patterns? No, it is the "culture" that must go first before the poor can be given what everybody else already possesses and many of us take for granted. In short, the poor must become "middle class," perhaps through "psychiatric treatment," and then we shall see what can be done about their poverty.

This is indeed the "social-work solution," as Lewis calls it. The only alternative to it is revolution, and that is allowable only far from home in backward countries where there are not enough psychiatrists and social workers to go around. Even there, the chief interest in revolution is that it may change the culture, whether or not it relieves material want.

The message to our own lumpenproletariat at home is thus to be relayed through those reliable channels, the policymakers, service administrators, and welfare workers: there are two choices, to become middle-class (without money) or revolt—and since revolts are allowed only in faraway places, the one acceptable solution becomes obvious. This scale of priorities, incidentally, has the further consequence that the many Americans who behave with middle-class respectability, or who fall into the category "stable working class," but still remain *poor*, can be ignored by those who run the "war against poverty." The plight of these people clearly has a low priority because it is more important to root out the last vestiges of the "culture of poverty" among the remaining lumpenproletariat. The prospect would seem to be that members of the lower class will all eventually graduate to the stable working class where they can then safely be ignored. By the time everyone in the Western developed nations has given up poverty culture to become both "stable" and "working," the rest of humanity will probably be about ready for the social workers and the psychiatrists to go to work on them. That is, they will probably have gotten the revolutionary bug out of their systems and reached a more developed stage. These projections make it possible to predict that we may never have to deal with the problem of poverty at all, at least within the foreseeable future. This is probably a good thing for our moral fiber because, as we have seen, poverty is a relatively easy problem, which means that winning out over the *culture* of poverty is a greater challenge.

Now care must be taken not to read too much into a few brief passages. So let us return to the literal meaning of our sources. Lewis says that the social-work-cum-psychiatry approach of altering the behavior of the poor is "the major solution" for problems connected with poverty in the United States. This is no different in essence from the writings by sociological and other proponents of "lower-class culture" which indicate, either by implication or quite bluntly, that the poor must first of all conform to conventional standards of respectability, until they find some way (none suggested) to eliminate their socioeconomic dependency. Thus the twin concepts, "culture of poverty" and "lower-class culture," have essentially identical implications in relation to major issues of public attitudes and policies. The salient common element is the insistence on absolute priority for doing away with the perceived behavioral, or "cultural," distinctions of the lower class. When one asks what could be the source of this insistence, a likely possibility seems to be a conviction that the behavior of the unworthy poor is dangerous and threatening. Is this anything other than a defensive projection of the values and interests of the middle class?

With respect to Lewis' work in particular, this is by no means a simple, unqualified theme, nor is it even an especially prominent element in his writing. Indeed, as we have seen, other aspects of these works seem quite inconsistent with this theme. Nevertheless, when Lewis more or less directly confronts policy questions, particularly concerning domestic problems in the United States, he does seem to violate his own humane values. These philosophical tenets are closely tied up with the generic anthropological idea of culture. If I have correctly interpreted the value conflict expressed in this work, I believe it is closely related to Lewis' intellectual problems with the culture concept. My feeling is that these quite real and perfectly legitimate doubts, in areas of technical method and scientific concept, eventually led to propositions with most unfortunate ramifications both in theory and in the realm of values. Having largely abandoned the classical culture concept initially, and having neglected some aspects of ethnographic method as a corollary to this theoretical shift, Lewis was therefore ill prepared to reinvoke culture for his larger model. His view of his subjects' lifeways became partial because of the relatively limited focus of his field techniques.

Toward the end of developing his abstract model, Lewis seems to arrive at the essence of the "culture of poverty," though this is not stated explicitly. He compares the lifeways of groups that have the "culture of poverty" with those of other groups that are poor but do not have such a "culture," and still other groups that have gotten rid of the poverty culture as he sees it. The essence remaining to distinguish the first category from the other two seems to consist largely or wholly of negative qualities, lacks, and absences. Group disintegration, personal disorganization, resignation, fatalism, and lack of purposeful action seem to be the major traits that finally distinguish the unregenerate poverty culture. This is indeed a singularly unprepossessing collection of attributes. If one could truly find a human mode of existence characterized only by these traits, it might be something like the chronic patient population in the back ward of a state mental hospital. It would certainly be difficult to grant such a collectivity much respect or high valuation as a human creation. Indeed, it might be quite easy to perceive this existence in terms of traditional negative stereotypes deeply embedded in one's own culture—and to feel threatened by it. The question that still remains difficult to answer is why Lewis was not disabused of this caricature by the autobiographies, which plainly portray a great deal of quite sanely organized and purposeful human life.

BREAKING WITH TRADITION AND RETURNING TO THE DARK GHETTO: KENNETH CLARK

As we saw in chapter 1, a minority of scholars have been expressing doubts for some time about the prevailing formulations of class cultures and poverty culture. Several books appearing in the middle 1960's may herald a general reassessment of these formulations. None of the works so far available deals with the whole problem. None has yet presented a full-scale alternative intellectual framework. Nevertheless, several have raised searching questions about the supposed cultural distinctiveness of disadvantaged communities and collectivities as presently understood by social scientists and others.

One important source of such queries is the recent research by Kenneth Clark and his associates in Harlem. This work was conceived as a study of disorganization and powerlessness. One finds in it some of the same problems of inappropriate methods and inadequate data repeatedly identified as other studies were discussed in earlier chapters. At the same time, however, certain key elements found in earlier research and writings are absent here. The classbound moralistic derogation of the Frazier tradition is one missing element. Another is the device of wrapping up the whole problem of lower-class life in the neat conceptual package of a self-contained cultural system which distracts attention from the impingements and impositions of the wider society. Being relatively free of these conceptual blinders enables Clark to raise some challenging issues.

The research carried out in Central Harlem under Clark's direction relied on census data, city agency reports, questionnaires, group discussions, and depth interviews. The resulting descriptions of "The Harlem Community" and "The Social Dynamics of the Ghetto" reflect quite straightforwardly both the strengths and limitations of their sources. This can be seen especially well in the Haryou Report, *Youth in the Ghetto*, which is the more extensive of two major works to come out of this research. The first descriptive chapter is unpretentiously titled "Demographic Characteristics." Here we find the familiar portrayal of "disorganization" and "instability" in terms of census figures on separation, single-parent households, and illegitimacy as well as statistics from the same sources on health, housing, occupation, and income. Then comes a chapter on "Community Pathologies" presenting quantitative data from city agencies on delinquency, crime, addiction, venereal disease, and welfare rates, together with a correlational analysis of interrelationships among these variables or "indices of pathology." Three additional chapters present similar descriptions and analyses of public education, employment patterns, and community social services. Finally, a section is devoted to verbatim selections from interviews, predominantly expressing attitudes of alienation and despair.

The distinctiveness of Central Harlem is repeatedly demonstrated by comparing one numerical index from Harlem after another with statistical norms for New York City as a whole and, by implication at least, with wider American norms. Kenneth Clark and his associates were clearly aware that such information and analysis—though certainly necessary—were neither sufficient nor adequate for their aim of understanding the Harlem community. "The statistical facts about Central Harlem . . . have been known for a long time. What the bare facts . . . fail to reveal, however, are the human anguish and sense of powerlessness that lie behind them."[1] This deficiency is partly remedied by presenting much verbatim

interview material. Moreover, one finds in the writings that
emerged from the research an authentic sense of compassion,
without sentimentality, and convincing indications that the
research workers were in close contact with at least some of
their human subjects—qualities certainly less evident in other
works reviewed earlier.

Yet something important is still lacking. A major deficiency
is that the Harlem community is still not presented in terms
of its *own* social order, cultural idiom, or life style. Even the
interview records have the ring of Harlemites self-consciously
presenting themselves to an outsider who, with his micro-
phone and tape recorder, has approached them with questions about what they think of "the problems" or "conditions" of Harlem. Such presentations no doubt add significantly to the statistical data. Yet they do not really overcome
the fact that Harlem is being described less in its own right
than by comparison with everything in America that is non-
Negro and non-slum. To return to household patterns, the
principal points made in the Haryou Report are that Harlem
has proportionally more separated spouses than New York
City as a whole, more children under 18 not living with both
parents, and more persons not living in families at all. Informants in interviews support this picture and comment on
associated difficulties with respect to parental discipline and
intergenerational communication. Yet we get little or no
portrayal of how these statistically deviant households actually function, what social processes go on within or between
them, or how they may be linked to other social units. They
are simply labeled "disorganized" and "unstable" because
they deviate from normative patterns of organization and
stability.

The question whether this community might have its own
distinct forms of social organization has hardly been posed
and could not be answered from the kinds of data presented.
The comparative structuring of the evidence insures that the
distinctiveness of social statistics from Harlem will be inter-

preted only as departures from general American norms. Thus the possibility of sociocultural coherence specific to Central Harlem is automatically ruled out by the frame of reference within which data are gathered and analyzed. It is as if a scholar set about describing and interpreting the distinctiveness of American society simply by comparing social statistics from the United States with norms for England or for the English-speaking world in general, using the known forms of British social structure as the standard of social order. Such a scholar would be bound to find many indications of "disorganization" in his American data. If he were a sensitive and humane individual, he might visit the United States to interview some of its citizens and discuss the "problems" and "conditions" of their social existence with them. This would probably give him further insights into the "instability" of American society, and some of these insights might be valid. Yet if our imagined scholar did no more than this, he might well leave the United States without ever grasping the fact that America has some forms of social order that do not exist in England or elsewhere in the English-speaking world.

While one hopes they do not exist in the world of serious scholarship, such commentators and visitors to the United States are of course not totally figments of fantasy. There are at least two major reasons why they are a vanishing type. First, America is obviously much too wealthy, powerful, and successful to be dismissed simply as an unstable deviant offshoot of British society. Second, the unique patterns of American society have long been extensively portrayed and interpreted in a huge body of art and scholarship that itself is both a creation of American culture and part of a developing international culture. By contrast, of course, the Harlems within America are neither wealthy nor powerful in the American context, and they are only beginning to portray themselves or communicate their own patterns through media that are understandable to the outside world of white, middle-class America. Perhaps this helps to explain how commentators and visitors from the larger America, including some who are both sophisticated intellectually and genuinely sympathetic toward the denizens of the "Dark Ghetto," persist in viewing this ghetto in terms of external criteria alone. In a different but not irrelevant context, ethnography has proved the key to understanding the internal coherence of other "deviant" social systems. Hence the thesis of this essay—that America needs an ethnography of its poor and its minorities.

Despite all that was said above in criticism of Kenneth Clark's work on Harlem, this man is one of the few students of lower-class Negro life who have begun to break the spell of the Frazier tradition. Clark himself makes it clear in a moving personal introduction that his return to the Dark Ghetto of his own origins was a poignant experience. He learned that

> To understand Harlem, one must seek the truth and one must dare to accept and understand the truths one does find . . . its paradoxes, its ironies, its comic and its tragic face, its cruel and its self-destructive forces, and its desperate surge for life . . . above all . . . its humanity. The truth of the dark ghetto is not merely a truth about Negroes; it reflects the deeper torment and anguish of the total human predicament.[2]

Clark reached these conclusions through his role as "an involved observer," which he recognizes "has much in common with . . . the methods of the cultural anthropologist." His important insights, however, have not received the recognition they deserve. He was apparently the first to recognize and demonstrate that "the cult of cultural deprivation" is "seductive" rather than insightful or productive. He understood that the cultural-deprivation approach all too easily serves as one more of the "subtle forms of social class and racial snobbery and ignorance," and that it thus becomes "an alibi for educational neglect" and so contributes to "the perpetuation of inferior education for lower-status children, whether their lower status is socio-economic or racial."[3]

Clark also understands that there is health and strength in the Dark Ghetto as well as the opposites of these qualities. On the basis of this recognition, he and his associates proposed ameliorative projects in which "it was *not* the primary objective of these programs to bring these youngsters into a 'helping' relationship with the case worker, group worker, or remedial specialist." The purpose was rather to encourage constructive subcultural change through "an esprit de corps and a tradition of effective social participation." "The Haryou's program planning placed its stress upon a restructured culture, or a new way of life, rather than upon a therapy."[4] Moreover, Clark is unlike the arrogant and patronizing commentators who advise communities like Harlem to solve their problems by "self-improvement," as if none of their difficulties stemmed from external influences. Clark's program also includes demands for change in major institutions which mediate the contacts and connections between the disadvantaged community and the wider society, particularly the public school system.

It does seem probable that a more ethnographic approach to understanding existing culture patterns in Harlem would have produced a sounder basis for programs to induce subcultural change. Such an approach might, for example, have discovered more positively adaptive patterns already functioning in the community to balance the rather heavy awareness of pathology pervading the Haryou documents. This might also have led to remedial projects with a less contrived, middle-class sound about them, less an air of being imposed from the outside, than the Cadet Corps, Junior and Senior Academies, coffee shop management programs, and so forth. Be all this as it may, however, there is no doubt that the dominant quality of interpretations and proposals alike in Clark's work belongs to a different world view than the Frazierian orientation.

BLACK CULTURE FROM THE BLUES TO
  HEAD START: CHARLES KEIL

It has been shown repeatedly in our discussion of prominent
writings on the poor that an important underlying source of
bias in these writings is an unexamined and strongly negative
value-judgment about the culture of the lower-class poor.
Within the intellectual ferment associated with the national
crisis surrounding poverty, one reaction to this negative
evaluation is an enthusiastically positive partisanship in
favor of lower-class lifeways and the people who follow them.
This value-position is not expressed only in contexts of political activism or advocacy of group interests. It can also be
found in works of scholarship. One notable piece of social
science writing that displays this point of view in scholarly
form is *Urban Blues* by Charles Keil. This work is largely
devoted to Negro male musicians in the entertainment business. The main body of the book is a unique description,
documentation, and analysis of the blues man, his place in
the entertainment world and in the ghetto, and his expressive
role with respect to the Negro "soul" complex.

Keil's main text stands between an introductory theoretical
essay on "urban lower-class Negro culture" and a concluding
peroration on the future of "the Negro problem." These
parts of the book demonstrate that a positive value-position
is not enough to resolve many of the difficulties that exist in
more conventionally oriented writing on disadvantaged
groups. From the start Keil falls into the basic difficulty of
extending his theoretical model well beyond the quite restricted range of his ethnographic data, making yet another
attempt to portray a whole culture. His main concern is to
replace the picture of "Negro culture" as disorganized and
pathological with a positive vision of a valid and valuable
"Negro culture." Yet Keil actually produces a general portrayal containing very little that is new, and thus what he has
changed is mainly the emotional valence and value tone with
which the same old alleged distinctions are presented.

Keil identifies the target of his wrath as the idea that "the Negro has no culture or at least no viable culture worthy of attention." He continues, "From an initial assumption that the Negro is only an American, a long string of insults and injuries inevitably flows. Remove the assumption, recognize a Negro culture, and many of the alleged pathologies disappear while others become subject to new and difficult verification."[5] The traits invoked to define this culture are a melancholy inventory familiar from many other sources: "middle class values tend to be reversed in the Negro cultural framework"; male-female relations are one great "battle of the sexes" revolving around the matrifocal family which is "normative if not normal"; "the black man on the street corner . . . lives for the present and tends to drift with events"; Negroes "can recite a stream of conventional American values and beliefs" but seldom live by them; "the hustler (or underworld denizen) and the entertainer are ideal types representing two important value orientations . . . clever and talented enough to be financially well off without working";[6] and so on. Keil may well have made an important contribution in his study of the blues and blues performers. On the subject of life among lower-class Negroes in general he has added no new evidence, few new ideas, and a refreshing partisan attitude.

With this fresh touch, we find again that large abstractions founded on a narrow range of evidence show a quality of extravagance. Thus, matching the hyperbole of those against whom he is arguing, Keil contends that "Negroes are the only substantial minority group in America who really have a culture to guard and protect."[7] This exaggerated vision seems to support the prescriptions that Keil offers for the future. These are "revitalization of Negro culture," "community self-help and quality education," and achievement of a positive black identity. How are these goals to be achieved? First we are reminded of Malcolm X's famous point that not integration but freedom is both the issue and the answer. Then:

"Freedom is founded upon choice. Choice, in turn, rests upon trained, truth-seeking intelligence and a profound awareness of real alternatives. These qualities depend to a frightening extent upon the success or failure of the much talked about pre-school program, Operation Head Start."[8] Here we are surely in the presence of an irreconcilable contradiction. What are the virtues and strengths of this vaunted "lower class Negro culture" if it cannot even inculcate "truth-seeking intelligence" or "awareness of real alternatives" without being revitalized by Head Start? The confusion is compounded when we find Keil simultaneously inveighing against "compensatory education for cultural deprivation" as "a misguided effort by white men to make Negroes over in their own ugly image."[9] Surely our author must be aware that Head Start is one of many current programs designed to inculate a middle-class "culture" among the poor with the hope that so equipped they may eventually arise from their poverty. So, by whatever process of reasoning, we are again confronted with the stale clichés of what Oscar Lewis called the "social work solution."

Yet Keil even goes beyond this. He voices the hope that the "resynthesis" he advocates will produce "what white America wants . . . evidence that Negroes can stand on their own feet."[10] Appropriately enough, Eric Hoffer is cited in support of this formulation. Thus we find ourselves somehow transported, within a few short pages, from the seemingly radical doctrine of "militant self-helping soul brothers," that only lower-class Negroes "really have a culture," all the way back to the Frazierian position that the black poor will be saved by "taking on the folkways and mores of the white race," i.e., the middle class.[11] This surely takes us right back to where we began to survey the development of contemporary ideas about the poor some thirty years ago (cf. chapter 2, pp. 18–24). Can it be that the American consciousness of class, especially when confounded with racial considerations, is so contorted that even those who try hardest for a new and constructive view of the poor must end up with the same denigrating diagnoses and pusillanimous prescriptions? We shall have more than one occasion to return below to the melancholy topic of confusion between racial and class stereotypes, considering Keil's ideas again when an attempt is made in chapter 5 (pp. 121–27) to resolve this confusion.

Second Thoughts on the Primitive and the Violent: Thomas Gladwin

Further evidence of intellectual doubts and stirrings within the poverty-culture school of thought comes from recent writings by another anthropologist, Thomas Gladwin. First, in an article published in 1961 Gladwin expresses his uneasiness about Lewis' thesis by explicitly recognizing that the concept of a poverty subculture rests on an inadequate ethnographic basis. Thus in a footnote he points out that "it is legitimate to question whether multi-problem families viewed collectively, would constitute a subculture in the anthropological sense. . . . Adequate research data do not at present exist to answer the question conclusively, even if the semantics of the definition of a subculture were sufficiently clear to offer definitive criteria."[12] Yet without any further explanation, Gladwin nevertheless expresses his belief that "it is useful to consider the implications inherent in the concept of subculture as applied to the multi-problem family, whether or not this working assumption is subsequently validated." Here Gladwin was writing primarily for an audience of social workers in a symposium devoted to problems of poverty. Not only his title but the terms of his presentation in general make one feel the pressures of such a situation to produce "The Anthropologist's View of Poverty." This might help to account for his use of the subculture concept in spite of his own well-founded misgivings.

Once embarked upon this course, however, we find many familiar dubious conceptions appearing with seeming inevitability. We learn that the poor are "infecting the larger society with many social ills," that their "characteristic type of family organization" "makes emotional cripples of this group and thus perpetuates their ineffectiveness," and that their deviant life style creates "dysfunctional relationships between this group and the society in which it is embedded."[13]

Gladwin conceptualizes the problem of amelioration in terms of culture change. As we should by now perhaps expect, it is by no means the larger culture or total social structure that he means to change; it is only the subculture of the poor. In examining this subculture, he writes, "our task is to search for those attributes which are most amenable to permanent change and which will at the same time exert the most effective leverage on the group's total pattern of living." Through this formulation he seeks to reorient the approach of social workers to the poor: "The hard core must be looked upon as people who share a dysfunctional subculture, not as re-calcitrant clients of social agencies."[14] It seems doubtful whether there is any significant difference between these two formulations that might lead to any new practice by social workers.

Gladwin suggests two characteristics of the subculture that he believes constitute starting points for change. These are "first the degree to which this population believes it has any actual control over its destiny individually or collectively and secondly their orientation toward the future."[15] With respect to both these areas, Gladwin makes it quite explicit that he is interested only in the subjective perceptions of the poor and not at all in the question whether there may be an objective, realistic basis for these perceptions. It is quite consistent with this that the program for change he recommends under the label "community development" is essentially an effort to convince the poor that they *can* control their destiny and that they *do* have a future—not to bring these conditions to reality, but simply to convince people that they are so. "Only after this realization is achieved can long-term economic plans be undertaken" or other substantial changes be made in the real conditions of life. Why must the approach be along these lines? It is because the hard-core poor in America present the would-be community developer with even "more formidable problems than are found in a village in Africa." After all, "the African villagers share a functioning social organization which provides a framework for social action," while "our multi-problem families exist in an environment of fairly complete disorganization."[16]

The logic of this argument leads Gladwin, like other poverty-culture analysts, finally to explain and justify his proposals in terms of the public values, the political power, and the perceived self-interest of the middle class. He remarks that effective help for the poor must involve some degree of acceptance of them as "fellow human beings" by those who are not poor. Then he continues.

> To be realistic, this acceptance will not develop magically or through appeals to conscience. Power rests in the middle class. And we in the middle class are notoriously anxious and defensive in the presence of people whose way of life is more primitive and violent than our own. We are threatened, and hence our response is rejection, not acceptance. We can become accepting only if we believe that by so doing we will reduce the threat.
>
> Thus we come around to the final point: the necessity for a workable program which will effectively reduce the social threat which the multi-problem family poses—the threat of delinquency, of vice, and of violence. It is my conviction that such a program must be one of directed culture change, one which will change the way of life that lies at the core of the culture of poverty.[17]

So what was initially presented as a "subculture," which might be understood and dealt with rationally, soon turns out to be a life of "complete disorganization," and is ultimately presented as the threat of the "primitive and violent." The power-holding middle class cannot be expected to lessen their hostility toward the poor unless the latter cease being a "threat." This makes it "realistic" that the only solution is to change the poor—not to make them less poor but to make them less primitive and violent.

Such "realism" neatly rules out of consideration a series of challenging questions. To what extent is the conventional middle-class view of the poor factually accurate, and to what extent is it a myth with a paranoid tinge? Granting that the comfortable strata may feel threatened by their social inferiors, is it not equally important to understand how the affluent and the powerful threaten the poor? What justification, beyond the brute facts of the present distribution of power, is there for the rather arrogant middle-class assumption that the lower class must make itself "acceptable" before it can share the material and psychic satisfactions of living in a wealthy and supposedly egalitarian society? Why do the architects of community development and social engineering never propose a "program of directed culture change" for the society as a whole, much less for its middle or upper strata, but only for the poor and powerless? Is "acceptance" really the primary change that the poor either need in some objective sense or desire subjectively? Is it not possible that some other indices of equality—say money or power—may have a higher priority for people who live in poverty? If this should be the case, what then will persuade the poor to seek harmony and "acceptance" by abandoning their subculture— the naked power of the police and the thinly veiled coercion of the social service agencies? If that is the answer, then we are obviously right back where we started, and all the intellectual paraphernalia of the subculture concept have gotten us nowhere.

Some of these questions must have bothered Thomas Gladwin since he wrote the paper just discussed. He has subsequently published a book, titled *Poverty U.S.A.*, in which he devotes thoughtful attention to a number of these problems. Unlike many of the works considered here, this is not a report of research but rather a collection of interpretive essays. The stated aim of the book is to define the problem of poverty in a tractable form. Yet the author does not allow the attractiveness of this goal to seduce him into presenting merely another recipe for changing the subculture of the poor. His conclusion is quite explicit.

> Therefore, if there is a central argument to this book it is that the social reforms necessary to make poverty avoidable and remediable must embrace a larger part of society than just the poor alone, and that these reforms can be implemented only by forces greater than those conceivably available to poor people, however well organized. These reforms must furthermore reallocate power, and above all money and the power that flows from money, within our society or else the poor will remain forever poor.[18]

It is not entirely clear that Gladwin is going to reach this conclusion until near the end of his book. A large part of the book is an intellectual wrestling match with the idea of poverty subculture and its policy implications, particularly in the recent "war on poverty." Gladwin does not himself present his work in these terms, but I believe this is a fair interpretation of it. Curiously enough, he does not mention his earlier doubts about the empirical basis and the semantics of the subculture concept. He seems to take it for granted that available descriptions of the "culture of poverty" are essentially valid. This assumption is epitomized by one of his chapter headings: "Poverty Is Being Incompetent."

Nevertheless, in another chapter titled "Poverty Is Being Despised" Gladwin clearly points out that the subculture concept all too easily becomes the basis for negative stereotypes quite inimical to the interests of the poor, especially when it is associated with an already despised ethnic category. "The idea of a culture, in this case a Negro culture, provides a neat pseudoscientific package of attributes against which to erect a barrier of discrimination. In this context attention has been directed especially at the Negro family and its breakdown."[19] A little further on he notes that "the current spate of literature on lower-class family life principally documents Negro family breakdown. Thus once more the poverty problem and the stereotypes which go with it is converted into a Negro problem and laid at the door of Negro culture or, for the more biased, Negro racial psychology."[20]

These and other implications of the poverty-culture idea are crucial to Gladwin's analysis and evaluation of recent anti-poverty programs which take up a large part of his book.

> The whole conception of the War on Poverty rests upon a definition of poverty as a way of life. The intellectual climate in which it was nurtured was created by studies of the culture of poverty, notably those of Oscar Lewis . . . [These studies] provided the basis for programs at the national level designed very explicitly to correct the social, occupational, and psychological deficits of people born and raised to a life of poverty.[21]

This is followed by a comparison between the national anti-poverty policies of the 1930's and those of the 1960's. It is suggested that a key strategy of the New Deal was structural change, altering the distribution of money and power in the society as a whole. Gladwin notes that policies with such aims are largely absent from the "war on poverty" and explains this difference as resulting from the fact that poverty is now a minority phenomenon in the United States, most Americans being affluent and therefore not likely to perceive anything wrong with the basic socioeconomic system.

> Add to this that poverty is viewed nowadays more as a disabling way of life than as unbalanced income distribution and it should not come as a surprise that the current emphasis is on people and the development of their social competence rather than on structural change.[22]

Thus the idea of a poverty culture turns out repeatedly to stand in the way of social policies that might bring about the very changes in the total system that Gladwin eventually concludes are required. Yet he spends many pages approvingly analyzing and positively evaluating the federal programs founded on the pervasive notion of poverty-as-a-way-of-life. For example, he praises the doctrine of "maximum feasible participation" by the poor as a genuine attempt to reallocate power, and he describes the many job training projects as creative attempts to make the poor more competent. Nevertheless, when he finally comes to evaluate all these efforts in terms of results he finds little to celebrate.

> In the last analysis, however, if the War on Poverty is truly intended to cure the causes of poverty . . . the power of the poor fostered by its programs can be judged sufficient only if it is able to generate major, meaningful and lasting social and economic reforms in conformity with the expressed wishes of poor people. . . . If we adopt this standard it is extremely difficult to find even scattered evidence of success . . . the poor remain as poor as ever, and the "power structure" remains the place where the power actually lies . . . the concessions which have been wrung from the power structure in virtually all communities are so trifling as to be almost inconsequential.[23]

Such a portrayal of dismal failure naturally prompts a search for explanations. Here Gladwin first falls back on the "culture of poverty" itself as a cause of the failure, thus compounding the confusions within the doubtful propositions on which the unsuccessful programs themselves were founded. Because poor people are unsophisticated and have a limited view of the world, he suggests, they are unable to develop effective strategies for achieving community power. And they are psychologically crippled by negative identity feelings, "lack of motivation to strive," "inability to delay gratification or to plan ahead," and so on through the usual dreary catalog. Gladwin wonders why the federal programs, which he thinks are brilliantly conceived and sensitively carried out, have not succeeded in enabling the poor to overcome these obstacles. He never quite arrives at the hypothesis that the therapy may have failed because the diagnosis was wrong, though at times he does seem close to considering this possibility.

The reforms proposed by Gladwin are put forward as additions to the "war on poverty," not as replacements for it. First, he endorses the guaranteed income as a substitute for traditional welfare programs. Second, he suggests some new equivalent of existing programs of veterans' benefits as a mechanism for allocating resources for self-help and self-improvement to the poor. Third, he proposes that the service area of employment be expanded and rationalized in order to provide new job opportunities for poor people. These proposals fall somewhat short of a bold program to accomplish what Gladwin has said is necessary, namely a reallocation of power in our total social system, but they might be a step in that direction. These are at least measures designed for the straightforward purpose of placing substantial new resources in the hands of the poor.

LIFE OF THE POOR AS SEEN FROM A STREET
    CORNER: ELLIOT LIEBOW

With one more recent work we reach a point where several strands of skepticism and some alternatives to the "culture of poverty" come together in an important piece of research. This is Elliot Liebow's study of lower-class Negro men, *Tally's Corner*. Trained as an anthropologist, Liebow did most of the work for this book literally on one street corner in Washington, D.C. One intellectual influence behind this study was clearly the work of William F. Whyte, a sociologist whose participant-observational research led him to find a highly organized social structure in another "street corner society," an Italian-American slum in Boston, some years before the phrase "culture of poverty" was coined. Liebow's research was part of a program directed by Hylan Lewis, whose critical skepticism with regard to class-culture concepts applied to the poor was cited earlier in chapter 1.

Liebow's anthropological background led him to adopt an

ethnographer's approach to his subjects. He makes explicit and documents his uneasiness about the validity of data gathered among the poor by formal interview and questionnaire techniques. His own methods are described in the following terms.

> The present study is an attempt to meet the need for recording and interpreting lower-class life of ordinary people, on their grounds and on their terms. . . . The data were to be collected by participant observation . . . with the aim of gaining a clear, firsthand picture of lower-class Negro men—especially "streetcorner" Negroes—rather than of testing specific hypotheses. . . . the intention was frankly exploratory.[24]

Liebow spent more than a year working in this way with some two dozen men who regularly passed a great deal of their time on a particular corner. He visited with them at this spot at all hours and less often accompanied some of the men elsewhere. Liebow did not live in the neighborhood of his subjects, and his research was not designed as a community study. Nevertheless, it is clear from his book that he came to know his small group of men very well and followed out their networks of association with considerable thoroughness and in substantial depth. Moreover, the author is quite aware of the biases imposed by his method, such as the omission from his sample of men who spend all their time at work, at home, or elsewhere away from the street corner.

The lives of the streetcorner men are explored in terms of two main dimensions: employment and interpersonal relationships. Within the latter area of life principal attention is given to marriage, nonmarital sex relations, fatherhood, friendships, and related associational networks. As episode after episode is described and one life story after another emerges, all skillfully woven together into a coherent picture, one overwhelming impression builds up for each of the several contexts explored. The men of Tally's corner are continually presented with insurmountable failure: experiences of failure, expectations of failure, and more experiences that confirm the expectations.

The following brief quotations are but summary descriptions and convey much less than the full circumstantial and personal detail which fills the book.

> The streetcorner man is under continuous assault by his job experiences and job fears. His experiences and fears feed on one another. The kind of job he can get—and frequently only after fighting for it, if then—steadily confirms his fears, depresses his self-confidence and self-esteem until finally, terrified of an opportunity even if one presents itself, he stands defeated by his experiences, his belief in his own self-worth destroyed and his fears a confirmed reality.[25]

And in another context:

> Thus, marriage is an occasion of failure. To stay married is to live with your failure, to be confronted with it day in and day out. It is to live in a world whose standards of manliness are forever beyond one's reach, where one is continually tested and challenged and continually found wanting. In self-defense, the husband retreats to the streetcorner. Here, where the measure of a man is considerably smaller, and where weaknesses are somehow turned upside down and almost magically transformed into strengths, he can be, once again, a man among men.[26]

Yet even in the refuge of streetcorner associations:

> Friendship thus appears as a relationship between two people who, in an important sense, stand unrevealed to one another. Lacking depth in both past and present, friendship is easily uprooted by the tug of economic or psychological self-interest or by external forces acting against it.
>
> The recognition of this weakness, coupled with the importance of friendship as a source of security and self-esteem, is surely a principal source of the impulse to romanticize relationships, to upgrade them, to elevate what others see as a casual acquaintanceship to friendship, and friendship to close friendship. . . . It is as if friendship is an artifact of desire, a wish rela-

tionship, a private agreement between two people to act "as if," rather than a real relationship between persons.[27]

Much of this material might seem at first sight to be grist for the culture-of-poverty mill. The man who collected the data does not see it that way. Liebow's most important single point in his interpretive conclusion is that the men he studied experience their lives as devoid of success or satisfaction, and they see themselves as personifications of failure, precisely because they share the standards and criteria of the wider culture. Far from being a self-sustaining system, set off from the rest of society by cultural distinctions based upon historical continuity, the streetcorner world is an integral part of America, living in continual and painful awareness of dominant American values and sentiments.

> From this perspective, the streetcorner man does not appear as a carrier of an independent cultural tradition. His behavior appears not so much as a way of realizing the distinctive goals and values of his own subculture, or of conforming to its models, but rather as his way of trying to achieve many of the goals and values of the larger society, of failing to do this, and of concealing his failure from others and from himself as best he can.[28]

Consistent with his whole analysis, Liebow believes the central cause of the poverty he has studied is that our society does not enable the lower-class Negro male to earn a living and support his family. If the problem represented by these men is to be solved, they must be given economically valuable skills and full opportunity to use them. Equally, they and their women and children must be enabled to believe that the men can and will succeed in making a living. Liebow does not spell out detailed programs for achieving these aims. He evidently believes that national policies already in effect will succeed if sufficient determination and resources are invested in them. He does make it clear, however, that programs simply aimed at changing life styles among the poor will not do away with poverty.

Anthropological Studies of Complex Societies: Method, Perspective, and Prospects for New Understanding

ETHNOGRAPHIC METHODS AND MODELS

We have seen that culture, in the anthropological sense, and the ethnographic approach are inextricably intertwined. This is true in the historical sense that the concept and the method developed together. It is also true in the sense that ethnography is the major anthropological source of empirical information from which particular cultures are described and upon which the generic concept of culture has been founded. This is not to say that ethnographic field work is the only way to study cultural systems. It is true, however, that ethnography is the principal anthropological contribution to the study of living cultures as wholes. Few anthropologists would, I think, disagree with the view taken here that ethnography is the preferred basic approach for investigating unknown or imperfectly known cultures. It has seldom been abandoned or replaced in cultural anthropological research, unless direct access to the behavior of living human groups is impossible, as in archeology, in the reconstruction of so-called "memory cultures," or in studies of "culture at a distance."

Ethnographic methods were devised as a means for exploring a way of life by direct, intensive, personal exposure to its conditions of existence. This approach was originally worked out through field research among tribal peoples. The utility of these methods for producing systematic and integrated portrayals of tribal cultures has been recognized for several decades. Subsequently, ethnographic approaches were adapted to the study of peasant communities, and here too their scientific value is well established. Oscar Lewis was prominent among the anthropologists who worked out the application of ethnographic method to research on peasant cultures.

In earlier studies the classical ethnographic problem of discerning natural cultural systems within manageable limits was resolved with relative ease. Small, isolated societies with relatively homogeneous ways of life could be convincingly treated as independent units of study. For the last twenty years or so, however, it has been increasingly realized that modern anthropology faces a quite different situation in studying subsocieties and subcultures within large, complex social systems. Much recent anthropological literature is concerned with the problem of conceptualizing relationships between definable smaller units such as tribes, village communities, or peasant groups, and larger wholes such as urban centers, national states, or traditional civilizations. Lewis also contributed to these discussions. More and more anthropologists have carried out field studies focused on modernization, urbanism, or urbanization both in the developing nations of the non-Western world and in the developed industrial societies of the West. This work makes up a large part of what has come to be called the anthropology of complex societies.

These recent interests have tended to develop along lines that are consistent with preexisting theoretical divisions within anthropology. One such division is between social anthropology, developed more by British scholars than others, and cultural anthropology, stemming largely from American sources. The British school concentrates on social relations and social institutions, generally either ignoring culture or using that term narrowly as a label for ritual symbols and community values. American cultural anthropology, on the other hand, is generally committed to studying cultural systems as total ways of life understood more or less as the culture concept is defined above in chapter 1. So today we seem to have both a social anthropology of complex societies and a cultural anthropology of complex societies. As we shall see, however, the two are not as different in all respects as these designations might seem to indicate.

Among the most prominent contributors to the cultural anthropology of complex societies undergoing modernization have been Julian Steward and a substantial group of collaborators. The work of these scholars now covers a variety of Latin American, African, and Asian communities. The core of their research methodology remains the ethnographic community study aimed at discovering local cultural systems. At the same time, they have brought together much information that is national in scope: historical data, statistical evidence, and materials on supra-local institutions. By integrating information from these various sources they have sought to describe not only how one local way of life is related to another but also how the several local designs constitute subsystems related to the national institutions of the complex social system as a whole. It is noteworthy that, except for one study of elite families in Puerto Rico, each of the particular cultural systems studied at first hand has been associated with a non-urban community.

The major practitioner of urban cultural anthropology has been Oscar Lewis, at least since he began developing his idea of a "culture of poverty" in 1959. Early in this period Lewis pointed to the problems of method entailed by the shift to urban studies as he saw them. "This new subject matter calls for some modification in the research designs of anthropologists. . . . City dwellers cannot be studied as members of little communities."[1] Social anthropologists doing some of the first modern urban studies in other parts of the world at about the same time took a similar view. The principal expedient adopted and emphasized by Lewis, as we have seen, was to make the family his unit of study. The taped autobiographies of course bulk very large in the published results of this approach. If, however, one considers the entire battery of techniques employed by Lewis in his family studies, the combination is much the same as that of traditional ethnography plus the addition of psychological tests commonly adopted by many cultural anthropologists since the 1940's.

Thus the difference between Lewis' approach to urban studies and standard ethnographic field work does not lie mainly in the techniques used for gathering information. The major contrast is rather in the unit of study, and consequently in the range of behavior and variety of social or cultural contexts that are investigated directly. Typically or ideally at least, the ethnographer has aimed to encompass all major aspects and dimensions of social existence for his subjects. Even though Lewis' mode of publication has skewed the available results of his work in the direction of autobiographical evidence, it is probably fair to describe the research in its entirety as family ethnography, or perhaps as the ethnographic study of families. This differs from the ethnography of communities, societies, or cultures not so much in technique as in scale, comprehensiveness, and level of abstraction.

Comparable partial ethnographic studies are to be found in much of the recent anthropological literature on complex societies. Indeed, this is not without precedent in earlier research on tribal and village societies within the tradition of social anthropology, with which a good deal of the newer work is connected. That tradition included, for example, ethnographies of kinship and marriage and ethnographies of politics, which played an important part in the development of social anthropological theory. In the more recent literature on urban life and complex societies, however, the narrow focus on restricted social contexts has become well-nigh ubiquitous. Thus we now find ethnographies of social networks, kinship patterns, patron-client relations, voluntary associations, and action-sets. This may reflect the preoccupation with social and cultural phenomena, small in scale, that have sometimes been suggested as constituting anthropology's prime interest, or even the definition of its subject matter. Thus we find distinguished commentators on the "anthropological contribution to the study of complex societies" remarking again on the anthropologist's "interest in the small-scale" and then roundly declaring, "It is clearly accepted that a study of large-scale institutional frameworks such as the economic, or the administrative and political, falls to the lot of economists, political scientists and sociologists."[2] While this is a scholarly division of labor that many anthropologists, including this writer, would not accept, it is nonetheless an influential position in helping to rationalize the use of partial ethnography in studies of complex societies.

Anthropologists have not really been so willing and able to leave the larger picture entirely to other human scientists as these statements seem to indicate, however. Both in studying the developing nations and in other urban research, they have either carried out their own or used the results of others' broad social surveys, basic quantitative and statistical studies, and demographic research. In contemporary African studies, for example, various scholars have made it clear that the two mainstays of anthropological method have been the social survey and what has been referred to here as partial ethnography. On the one hand, these writers refer to "anthropological" approaches which "provide qualitative data based on 'free' or 'open' interviews combined with participant-observation over a relatively long period,"[3] "qualitative studies," and "intensive inquiry into cultural patterning and social institutions."[4] By these phrases I take it they mean ethnographic field work. According to J. Clyde Mitchell, anthropologists in modern Africa have added large-scale social surveys to their more usual techniques partly because few of the social statistics normally available in Western nations exist in Africa, but equally because they believe that social phenomena and data from towns or cities are too complicated to be dealt with successfully by traditional anthropological techniques.

It thus appears that in turning to studies of complex societies many anthropologists have not only narrowed their ethnographic focus; at the same time they have also begun to rely increasingly on the methods and findings of others, particularly sociologists, to sketch in the wider picture that is no longer examined ethnographically. Now it seems to me that Oscar Lewis has adopted precisely this twin methodological shift. In *La Vida*, for example, apart from the partial ethnography of the Rios family, the main sources from which the "culture of poverty" is portrayed seem to be social surveys carried out by Lewis and his associates, plus already available social statistics from Puerto Rico and New York.

There is one striking difference between Lewis' work and that of most other anthropologists engaged in the study of complex societies. The latter generally do not put forward broad theoretical constructs at a high level of abstraction transcending their narrowed ethnographic vision and comprehending the large-scale social phenomena portrayed through non-ethnographic methods. As far as I am aware, one does not find them suggesting any such abstractions as, let us say, a culture of recently detribalized urbanites, a new urban social structure, a single-pattern politics of developing nations, a culture of newly emerging social classes, or anything else comparable to the "culture of poverty." Instead, the anthropology of complex societies has typically produced rather small-scale theoretical concepts, such as social network, quasi-group, action-set, or attenuated affinality, that are quite appropriate to their rather narrow ethnographic reach. A methodological rationale for this restriction has been stated succinctly by Mitchell: "In this interaction between intensive and quantitative research it is likely that fruitful hypotheses will arise most frequently out of the insights acquired in intensive studies. The appropiate role for quantitative research is to test and refine these hypotheses rather than to generate them."[5]

Lewis obviously would not accept this formulation. He has by no means limited his hypotheses or his hypothetical abstractions to those generated from his intensive studies of poor families. Working within such a limitation would allow him only to offer a hypothetical family system of the poor, certainly not a "culture of poverty" supposedly comprehending all levels and aspects of lower-class life. Contrary to any such caution or rigor in method, Lewis has created a great overarching abstraction that not only depends heavily on sweeping interpretations of rather superficial quantitative data but even, as we have seen, fails to square with important aspects of his ethnographic evidence. Other anthropological students of complex societies may have unnecessarily and unfortunately narrowed the theoretical scope of their work by restricting their ethnographic focus. Lewis certainly seems, from all indications in his published materials, to have gone to the opposite extreme of building conceptual castles out of something all too close to empirical thin air.

SUBSOCIETIES AND SUBCULTURES: NEGLECTED DISTINCTIONS AND THE FAD OF "CULTURES"

Most social scientists who write about a way of life peculiar to the poor mention in passing that their subject is really only a "subculture" rather than a "culture" in the full sense. Few of these writers examine this distinction or explore its implications. Indeed, the most frequent practice is to use the term "culture" throughout after an initial reference to the distinction. This is a significant oversight because the difference between the two concepts, although a simple one, is not negligible. Clarity in this elementary matter might have averted some of the important difficulties in such notions as the "culture of poverty" and "lower-class culture."

Some of the confusion stems from a failure to specify systematically the nature of social units and their relationships to society as a whole. Clarification of these matters is very much overdue, if only because it has become so intellectually stylish to discover "cultures" everywhere in national and international life. Such "ways of life," "group traditions," "life styles," and so forth are now being seriously attributed to a congeries of human groupings which would be little short of astonishing if one considered them all together. An inventory amounting to a dozen sets of such social categories comes to mind after only brief reflection. The list only begins with (1) socioeconomic strata—such as the lower class or the poor. It goes on to include (2) ethnic collectivities —e.g., Negroes, Jews; (3) regional populations—Southerners, Midwesterners; (4) age grades—adolescents, youth; (5) community types—urban, rural; (6) institutional complexes—education, penal establishments; (7) occupational groupings —various professions; (8) religious bodies—Catholics, Muslims; and even (9) political entities—revolutionary groups, for example. Yet this does not exhaust the catalog, for one also finds (10) genera of intellectual orientation, such as "scientists" and "intellectuals"; (11) units that are really behavioral classes, mainly various kinds of "deviants"; and (12) what are really categories of moral evaluation, ranging from "respectables" to the "disreputable" and the "unworthy" poor.

Within each of these classes, any number of specific units have been loosely characterized as distinctive by virtue of various "culture patterns." Indeed, several kinds of literature, from popular journalism to academic writing, have become cluttered with such facile conceptualizations. Particularly in its more popular forms, the "culture of poverty" is thus part of a larger stream of ideas which has assumed the attributes of a fad. To cite but a small sample, besides (1) poverty culture, we now have (2) "Negro culture," such old standbys as "Jewish culture," and many more to go with these; (3) longstanding regionalisms like "the Southern way of life"; (4) "adolescent culture" or "teen-age ways"; (5) everything from "exurbanite life styles" to "slum culture"; (6) "the culture of schools" and the mental hospital as a "cultural system"; (7) medical, legal, and other professional "cultures"; (8) Muslim or Catholic "cultures"; (9) the "revolutionary way of life"; (10) the "two cultures" of physical science and literary intellectualism; (11) patterns for almost any deviance one cares to name, e.g., "thief subculture" and "convict subculture"; and (12) a rich lode of despicable low-life styles—with labels ranging from pithy derogations like "dregs culture" to learned euphemisms like "externally adapted culture" and conceptual absurdities like "the unsocialized."

Those of the social categories cited above that have at least a degree of coherence as collectivities within the larger social system may be regarded as subsocieties. They are strata, segments, or other constituent units within that larger system— the society as a whole. By definition, they are distinct from the total system only in the same logical sense that any part is differentiated from the whole in which it is embedded. While most discussions of such units emphasize their distinctness, it is obvious that structural articulations to the rest of the system, attributes shared with other subunits, and elements common to the society as a whole are equally real aspects of all subsocieties. It is perhaps reasonable to assume that any subsociety may have a configuration of more or less distinguishable lifeways of its own. This configuration constitutes a subculture that is distinct from the total culture of the whole society only in a correspondingly special and limited sense. The wider sociocultural system has its own coherence to which subsocieties and subcultures contribute even with their distinctiveness.

Speaking broadly, subcultures within a culture may be compared with dialects of a language. Regional, class, and generational subsocieties are often distinguished by linguistic variations, sometimes regarded as dialects, which are part of their subcultures. The differences between subcultures within a larger way of life may be similar to the contrasts in idiom, the limited differences of vocabulary, or accent found to differentiate dialects. Common structural principles and common elements of form and content shared by dialects make them recognizable as belonging to the same language. Similarly, subcultures presumably share some themes, patterns, and configurations marking them as parts of a culture. These common elements and principles generally enable subsocieties to coexist in organized interaction or predictable relations based on subcultural patterns, much as different dialects are often more or less mutually intelligible. The definition, analysis, and interpretation of dialects are by no means fully solved problems in linguistics. The study of distinctions, commonalities, and articulations among subcultures as well as investigation of their organization and functions is, if anything, considerably less well worked out.

In both fields, moreover, the lack of clear understanding is matched by the distortions of ignorance. Just as provincial and unsophisticated thought tends to misidentify a highly distinctive dialect as "a different language," so the class-bound and the status-conscious easily equate an unfamiliar or uncongenial subculture with "a different way of life." One finds little to clarify the central problem of subcultures either in the work of social scientists examined in earlier chapters or in the rhetoric of political and ideological debate. Practitioners of the various human sciences have written much on social stratification, intergroup relations, regional sociology, assimilation of immigrants, deviant behavior, and other relevant matters without greatly changing the status of the subculture as a problem for analysis. In wider public discourse we have not progressed much beyond the pious platitudes of "Americanism," such unvarnished sentimentalities as the "Southern way of life," the stale old chestnuts like "middle-class values," or the reactive assertions of "Black Culture." Nevertheless, the basic elements of a clear concept are available in some of the literature from the cultural anthropology of complex societies and one or two closely related sociological works.

DEFINITIONS AND CLARIFICATIONS OF THE CONCEPT OF SUBCULTURE

The idea of subculture has had a small but distinctive place in American anthropology for some time. Going back at least to the 1930's it appears in general discussions of the nature of culture by such major figures as Ralph Linton, A. L. Kroeber, and Melville Herskovits. The following passage by Kroeber is representative and succinct.

> We have seen how each class in a society exhibits a more or less distinct phase, a subculture of the total culture carried by the society; just as geographical segments of the society manifest regional aspects of the culture. This principle extends further: to age levels and the sexes. Men do not practice the specific habits of the women in their culture, and vice versa. ... At the same time these sex phases are never felt as constituting more than a side or an aspect of the culture—nor, indeed, do they constitute more ... the culture is not felt as complete, and is not complete without both components. The same thing holds, incidentally, for the class phases, and often for the regional phases of well integrated cultures. Scavengers and bankers will be recognized in such cultures as quite properly following diverse strains of life and making diverse contributions, but their coherence within the body politic of culture and society is felt to outweigh the separateness. They are both organs within the same body, like the patricians and plebians in the old Roman fable about the stomach and the limbs.[6]

Such statements may have been taken for granted by some of those who have written on poverty and the poor, but their implications have seldom been followed out and applied in such contexts. In particular, formulators of poverty cultures would have done well to follow Kroeber's stress on the complementarity of subcultural distinctness and total-culture coherence.

While no attempt is made here to trace the history of the concept in full, it has been used in various contexts between these early general statements and the current burgeoning interest in complex societies. In anthropological essays on the contemporary United States, for example, Conrad Arensberg delineated subcultures for a number of community types, and Evon Vogt set forth subcultures of Mormons and Texans respectively, viewing each as a historical continuum. The cultural heterogeneity of Latin America has been another source of interest in culturally distinct subsocieties. Taking this region as a whole, Charles Wagley and Marvin Harris put forward a classification of nine major subculture types, employing ethnic, ecological, community, and class criteria in various combinations. Partly because these two authors were presenting a regionwide typology rather than an integrated system, their discussion highlights the distinctness of subcultures rather than mutual articulations between subsystems. They also note that "although the urban proletariat is numerically the dominant segment of the metropolitan centers, it is the least well known of all" the subsocieties that they distinguish.[7]

The wide-ranging work of Steward and his associates, referred to earlier in this chapter, is partly an outgrowth of closely related Latin American research. Steward's most recent presentation of his conceptual framework includes the following lines.

> Subcultural group, subsociety, and social segment have been used to designate those social groups within a large society that are distinguishable by ethnic background, occupation, religion, race, status or other common characteristics and yet share certain features with other social segments. Subcultural groups or subsocieties within a certain nation all conform to national laws, they potentially acquire many culture elements of the national inventory, and they are influenced by national institutions. . . .
>
> The more meaningful diagnostics of a subcultural group are its structural features. These may result from tradition, from the effects of supracommunity institutions, and from interactions with other groups. The extent to which the effects of any particular structures, such as those pertaining to employment, religion, political affiliations, or associations . . . have some inner consistency is a matter of empirical investigation. Subcultural groups crosscut and interlock with one another in many respects. . . .[8]

Here we may note again several important aspects of the subculture concept which were conspicuously ignored or glossed over in many of the works on the poor reviewed in earlier chapters. First is the balanced attention to both subcultural distinctions and elements shared among different subsystems. Second is the explicit recognition that distinguishing structural characteristics may have sources that are either external or internal to the subsociety. Third is the insistence that the nature of subcultures, including their degree of distinctness, is a matter for empirical discovery.

Another cogent statement on subsocieties and their lifeways appears in Herbert Gans's *Urban Villagers*, a community study of the Italian-American poor in Boston. Gans belongs to a small group of American sociologists who practice many of the techniques of ethnography. His book resembles an ethnographic monograph in many aspects of approach and scope. Since Gans was probably influenced by intellectual traditions derived from social anthropology, his sensitivity to cultural issues is testimony to the artificiality of boundaries not only between disciplines but also between schools of thought within disciplines. Urban anthropologists seem to have evinced little interest in this work by Gans, a circumstance that may be in part a result of these same arbitrary boundaries. Perhaps the relevance of this work to research on the lower-class poor has been missed partly because Gans conceptualizes the lifeways he studied as a working-class subculture and explicitly contrasts this with lower-class patterns. From our present viewpoint, it is a pity that this perceptive observer did not study lower-class people at first hand, but his discovery of a slum community is nonetheless significant. To deny this discovery any relevance to problems of research on poverty subcultures would be again to prejudice our investigation by reliance on unproved assumptions about the nature of our subject.

Gans presents easily the most acute theoretical definition of classes as subsocieties, with associated subcultures, known to me. Social classes, he writes, are

> strata in the larger society, each of which consists of somewhat —but not entirely—distinctive social relationships, behavior patterns, and attitudes. The strata thus are composed of subcultures and sub-social structures. . . . While occupation, education, income, and other such factors help to distinguish the subcultures, the exact role of these factors is thought to be an empirical question. The strata are defined as subcultures on the assumption that relationships, behavior patterns, and attitudes are related parts of a social and cultural system. The word "system" must be used carefully, however, for many similarities and overlaps exist between them. Moreover, these systems are quite open, and movement between them is possible, though . . . not always easy. Considerable variation also exists within each stratum, for social mobility and other processes create innumerable combinations of behavior patterns.[9]

Thus elucidation of part-whole structural relationships is combined with recognition of internal heterogeneity. Here also we again find an insistence that the content and distinctiveness of subcultures must be regarded as questions to be settled empirically, a point further emphasized by Gans.

> The great advantage of the subcultural conception is that it makes no a priori assumptions about the major differences between the strata or the determinants of these differences. It treats them rather as topics for empirical research. Unlike the other approaches in which class is defined in terms of easily researchable indices, the subcultural conception is harder to employ, however, for the characteristics and determinants of each class subculture must be carefully delineated.[10]

If these sane and simple guidelines had been followed rigorously by others, from Frazier to Moynihan to Lewis, there would be no need for much of the negative criticism in this essay. It is precisely because Gans is one of the very few who have consistently recognized and applied these cautions that most existing ideas of poverty subcultures are in such serious need of empirical evaluation. Perfectly consistent is the further fact that Gans presents a Methodological Appendix that must take first rank as a concise, informative, and candid guide to the technical procedures, intellectual problems, and ethical dilemmas of observational and participant approaches in an urban setting. It must also be noted that *Urban Villagers* is a much more fully rounded subcultural community study of a local subsociety than any of the other works reviewed in chapters 2–4. The descriptive portions are not confined to households, social networks, or whatnot. The main topical areas covered include the family, peer groups, the community, work, education, health patterns, social services, politics, consumption, and mass media.

After describing the subsystem patterns emerging from this research, Gans evaluates working-class subculture on the basis of his own field work and then adds an evaluation of lower-class subculture based mainly on information available from the sociological literature. The contrast between the two judgments may be instructive. "It should be evident from the description of the West Enders in the previous chapters that I believe the working-class subculture to be a generally satisfactory way of adapting to the opportunities which society has made available."[11] "This is not true, however, of the lower-class subculture . . . it fails to succeed . . . breeds men who find it increasingly difficult to survive in modern society . . . many elements of lower-class life are not merely culturally different . . . but they are in fact pathological."[12] Would fully rounded ethnographic field work produce a more positive picture of life among the lower-class poor? We do not yet know, but it seems worthwhile to find out.

Another point made in the same discussion by Gans may be quite important. He suggests that lower-class Americans, women in particular, are so discontented and alienated from their mode of existence that they make a positive effort not to socialize their children into the lower-class subculture. "Lower-class women may not often succeed in raising their children to reject the culture they live in, but the mere fact that they try illustrates the absolute qualitative difference between the lower-class subculture and all the others."[13] If this striking and basic contrast does indeed exist, it suggests at least two interpretations which are not necessarily mutually inconsistent.

Such a pervasive disaffection from existing patterns of existence could mean that the American lower class, or perhaps segments thereof, are ripe for massive cultural revitalization, which could take the form of religious and/or secular protest movements. Several aspects of recent behavior by Negro ghetto groups obviously lend weight to this possibility. The other possibility is that lower-class life does not actually constitute a distinct subculture in the sense often used by poverty analysts, because it does not embody any design for living to which people give sufficient allegiance or emotional investment to pass it on to their children. That is, whatever is distinctive about lower-class life may be no more than a situational adaptation to the structural position of the bottom stratum in a highly stratified society. Accordingly, it is possible that the poor may be much more "middle-class" or "working-class" in their values, aspirations, and other cultural orientations than previous research has indicated. It may also be that the experience of living in poverty produces classbound behavior patterns without distinctive values and in spite of parental efforts. Existing information does not enable us to do more than pose these questions. Once again ethnographic studies seem highly advisable as a step toward clarifying these issues.

WHEN IS A "CULTURE" NOT A CULTURE?

In this discussion we have noted a number of contemporary challenges presently facing the human sciences in general and anthropology in particular. The problem of the subculture should be added to these. Perhaps anthropology, as the discipline that contributed most to making the culture concept a seminal idea in modern thought, can make another contribution here. Some preliminary consideration toward this end can be suggested by further examining the poverty-culture idea. One of the major weaknesses of this notion as so far presented by Oscar Lewis is its failure to produce clarity on this very problem. We may begin by adopting the working hypothesis that the lower-class poor constitute a subsociety of the modern Western social system in general and of the United States social system in particular. This seems a plausible starting point in view of the findings in two sizable bodies of literature: the long-established sociological tradition of studies of stratification and the more recently emerging, broadly eclectic literature on American poverty. Our working hypothesis enables us to ask one major research question and to pose a series of derived or subsidiary queries. The master question must be, does the lower-class subsociety have a distinguishable subculture of its own? Other issues would include the following. What elements or patterns of this subculture are distinctive? What culture traits or configurations are shared by the lower class with the middle class or with the system as a whole? How is the subculture articulated with the whole culture? In lower-class life, should comparable but contrasting subcultural and wider cultural traits be understood as mutually exclusive, coexisting alternatives, or in some other relationship? How are distinctive patterns perpetuated? Are shared patterns perpetuated by similar means in different subsystems? What functions, adaptive or otherwise, do subcultural configurations have?

These questions can be thoroughly answered only by investigating and describing at first hand the entire range of custom and belief that make up the whole culture of representative lower-class populations. The most direct approach to such research would clearly be fully rounded ethnographic studies among the poor. In the study of any subsociety, obviously, an important objective is to determine in what ways its subculture is distinctive. This has indeed been the major goal of most of the published research cited here. It is clear, however, that equally important aims are to discern what cultural features are shared by different but related subsystems, and how subcultures are articulated with universals in the total system. These are the research tasks and analytical problems that have received so little attention, particularly with respect to lower-class subculture. These aspects of the problem have generally been swept under the rug by the expedient of treating distinctively lower-class traits as distortions, incomplete versions, or pathological variants of middle-class patterns. In contrast, an ethnographic approach would aim to comprehend lower-class life as a whole and thus would devote as much attention to cultural commonalities as to contrasts and discontinuities. This is necessary simply because the definition of distinctiveness is quite dependent on an understanding of what is not distinctive.

Hardly separable from the problems of the existence and distinctiveness of a subculture is a further question: whether many of the features presented by Lewis and others as class-distinctive traits are really culture patterns at all. Lewis defines his model of poverty culture as describing "a way of life handled on from generation to generation" which "provides human beings with a design for living," and he correctly notes that this corresponds to "a culture in the traditional anthropological sense."[14] Yet within his catalog of traits are quite a number that fit into this definition with difficulty, if at all. Many of these features seem more like externally imposed conditions or unavoidable matters of situational expediency, rather than cultural creations internal to the subsociety in question. From the list of poverty-culture traits we can abstract three categories of elements posing different sorts of questions for each of these problematical issues. The sets of items here selected from Lewis' trait list are placed in categories designed for present analytical purposes, rather than Lewis' own classification of the traits.

The first set of items consists of *gross indicators or correlates of poverty.* These include unemployment, underemployment, unskilled work, low-status occupations, meager wages, lack of education, crowded living quarters, and deteriorated housing. Whether these phenomena can be correctly understood as parts of a "design for living" "handed on from generation to generation" through socialization seems open to doubt. As we noted earlier, Lewis himself insists on the distinction between poverty and the "culture of poverty." Are these phenomena not better understood as conditions or symptoms of being poor rather than as inculcated patterns of social tradition? Another of Lewis' own formulations may sharpen the issue: he describes culture as "a ready-made set of solutions for human problems." The question can thus perhaps be rephrased: Are unemployment, low wages, and so forth better understood as problems or as solutions for problems?

Lewis, together with the expositors of lower-class subculture, seems to believe that these are the lower-class cultural solutions to the basic bioeconomic problem of survival. Furthermore, they contend that these "solutions" are part of the lower-class "design for living" in the sense that they are supported by subcultural values and attitudes and perpetuated by personality traits that result from lower-class socialization patterns. The alternative interpretation is that lack of work, lack of income, and the rest pose conditions to which the poor must adapt through whatever sociocultural resources they control. That is, these conditions are phenomena of the environment in which the lower class lives, determined not so much by behaviors and values of the poor as by the structure of the total social system. It may be suggested also that this larger structure is perpetuated primarily by the economic and political actions of the non-poor. Then we may view behaviors and values peculiar to the poor as responses to the experience of their special socioeconomic environment and as adaptations to this environment. Moreover, this view does not require that distinctive socialization patterns or personality configurations be invoked to explain class-specific beliefs and practices, a point to which we shall return.

Evidence presented in the literature surveyed here seems to provide little basis for a clear choice between these interpretations. To conclude that the two formulations are both valid but not mutually exclusive—that the two causal sequences may be coexistent and perhaps mutually reinforcing—is a position that may ultimately prove well founded. In the present state of the evidence, however, this conclusion has the ring of an evasive eclecticism. New evidence must be found, and much of it can be discovered through ethnography. Much of the answer must come from on-the-spot observation and inquiry into how people actually treat the conditions in question during their daily lives, under both usual and unusual circumstances. Much can be learned about the extent to which people develop and practice individual or collective means for coping with the conditions as problems potentially susceptible to resolution—or, conversely, the ways in which people may learn to accept these conditions as a normal part of the best or only available mode of existence. In the course of such inquiry, much would also come to light on the distinctiveness of lower-class cultural responses.

The second group of traits found in the subcultural model presented by Lewis consists of *behavioral patterns and relationships*. These include practice of consensual marriage, high frequency of female-centered households without resident adult males, absence of a sheltered childhood, authoritarianism in family relationships, lack of family solidarity, and general failure to develop community organization beyond the household. These examples are typical of the whole list in their emphasis on lacks and absences. Such characterizations convey an impression, not of distinctive subcultural patterns, but rather of a highly random, unpatterned social existence. "Indeed," writes Lewis himself in a frankly evaluative passage, "the poverty of culture is one of the crucial aspects of the culture of poverty."[15]

Nevertheless, it seems most unlikely that this culturally barren set of behavioral and relational traits is really intended to be an exhaustive portrayal of social organization among the poor. To begin with, one can again infer from the emphasis on subcultural distinctions that the role of total-system universals has been neglected or perhaps virtually ignored. Also, this is an area in which Lewis' great concentration on family data has probably led naturally to a lack of information on other aspects of social structure. Moreover, there may be many contexts in which relationships or groupings that seem lacking in organization are actually functional adaptations to the circumstances of poverty. Lewis touches on a few of these, such as the advantages of free unions over marriage for the very poor, but there may be many more. An ethnographic attempt to master the whole shape of social existence from within is needed to clear up these and many related questions. That is, it is most necessary for ethnographers studying the poor to look for forms of social organization and patterned relationships that Lewis does not report.

With respect to the relationships and group forms that do appear in Lewis' trait catalog, it is often quite difficult to decide from available information whether these are sanctioned and perpetuated by subcultural values and beliefs that are communicated through socialization. In some cases at least, it seems quite possible that they are situational adaptations with little or no specific subcultural rationale. Wherever this is the case, the social practices involved may stem from motivations that are consistent with value orientations common to the total culture but capable of only distorted or incomplete expression within the limits of a poverty environment. Whatever behavior can be so interpreted may be better understood as an artifact of the total system rather than a response to subcultural rules or standards.

The third set of elements that can be drawn from the trait list associated with the "culture of poverty" belongs to the realm of *values and attitudes.* Here one is struck first of all by a long series of hostile feelings toward institutions and power centers of the dominant classes. Also found here is a substantial list of negative feelings which the poor are said to harbor toward their own group and its place in the social structure. These elements can be summed up as a combination of potential for protest, together with low levels of expectation and aspiration. Various expressions of spatial and temporal provincialism are also emphasized. All these orientations are so strikingly consistent with objective situational factors that it seems hardly necessary to interpret them as ingrained subcultural values. Indeed, for modern Western people these would seem to be almost inevitable emotional responses to the actual conditions of poverty.

A few suggestions of articulations between the subculture and more general values of the total system are advanced by Lewis. Thus he states that people with poverty culture "claim as their own" some middle-class values with respect to marriage but do not practice these values. He further suggests that one finds a "verbal emphasis upon family solidarity" also not lived up to in reality. He notes a few specific values that, it seems to me, have a definite place in dominant American traditions, quite apart from any lower-class subculture. These include a sense of neighborhood community and a belief in male dominance. All this seems far from adding up to a separate subsystem of values. It would certainly be difficult to find in this catalog a sufficient body of subcultural value orientations to provide rationales and sanctions for all the distinctive traits set forth in other aspects of social life. It seems that much remains to be specified here. The operative patterns still to be discovered may turn out to be some combination of total-system themes and class-specific values. Many of these can be specified through ethnographic research combining observation of much behavior with many recorded expressions of attitudes, both solicited and spontaneous.

One further consideration has received little attention in the relevant literature, probably because the stress on subcultural distinctiveness has inhibited its exploration. This is the possibility that commitment to values, norms, and other cultural themes may often involve ambiguity, ambivalence, and the simultaneous holding of alternative or contradictory beliefs. Some of these possibilities are suggested by Rodman's ingenious idea of "value-stretch." Lee Rainwater has recently followed this up by exploring thoughtfully how "conventional society manages somehow to inculcate its norms even in those persons who are not able to achieve successfully in terms of them," including groups who are thought to live within a poverty subculture.[16] This consideration needs empirical development through ethnographic field work so that we may see more clearly how subcultural elements and total-system universals can coexist as simultaneously available alternatives.

Such investigation may free us from the strain—so evident in the literature—of explaining all class-specific behavior in terms of putative or hypothetical sets of subgroup beliefs and values. These suggested lines of inquiry may also make it easier to perceive and appreciate how cultural resources of various proveniences may be flexibly combined in creative responses to the imperative of adaptation under stressful circumstances, including the deprivations of poverty. Hopefully such reflections may weaken the now seemingly well-nigh tyrannical power of the association between poverty and pathology in the minds of social scientists concerned with understanding their own social system. If this point is reached, the way will be open for field investigations more free of preconceptions and therefore more likely to produce a valid picture of social and cultural order in the life of the poor. An integral part of this approach must surely be critical attention to the nature of subsocieties and subcultures.

ETHNIC GROUPS, SOCIAL CLASS, AND POVERTY

Our discussion of subsystems reminds us that in a complex society it is possible to identify many separate dimensions of structural differentiation, each of which may also involve a continuum of subcultural variation. More or less distinguishable social categories at different points on these many dimensions constitute a great variety of subunits variously interrelated. All this is presumably at least part of what we mean when we describe a social system as complex. In order to understand such a system thoroughly, it is of course necessary to examine as many of these subunits on different dimensions as possible. If we take our structural definition of subsocieties seriously, a full understanding of any one stratum or segment will require considerable elucidation of the larger system within which it is embedded. It follows that to understand one subsociety we must inquire into the nature of many other subunits related to the main subject in various different ways. The primary dimension of relationship between social categories is the dimension defining the categories themselves, such as relations of social class to social class or of one age grade to another. There are also secondary interrelations which cut across these dimensions, such as the frequently complex interplay among class, ethnic group, age grade, and others.

The lower-class poor as a subsociety are by definition of course a socioeconomic stratum. As such, their place in the whole system is defined primarily by their relationship to other strata, among which at least the working class, the middle class, and an upper class are commonly distinguished. Thus discussions of the poor generally involve much explicit or implicit reference to these other categories of stratification, and at least implied comparison with them. The additional, secondary dimensions of substructural and subcultural differentiation can then be examined in terms of their relevance to the lower class as such. The secondary dimensions of differentiation will be relevant in two different ways. First, they will define some internal variations or heterogeneity within the lower class. Second, they will differentiate various aspects of the rest of society, each of which impinges on the lower class in some particular way. Both are taken into account, to some extent at least, in the more comprehensive models of life among the poor, such as Lewis' "culture of poverty." Among the traits in Lewis' model there are, first, a number which refer to internal differentiation of the lower class, including sex roles, age statuses, and occupational differences. Lewis also takes some account, second, of varying relationships between the poor and external institutions, agencies of social control, community services, political groups, and so on. Future ethnographic research should further improve our understanding of these complexities.

One dimension of subsystem variation, commonly viewed as secondary to social class, is particularly important to students of culture and has an especially confused status in the poverty literature. This is ethnic group membership. Some general discussions of the poor make no reference to ethnicity. Broad treatments of poverty in America do often stress the fact that ethnic minorities are disproportionately represented among the poor. While such discussions often clarify the discriminatory disadvantages suffered by Negroes or other particular categories, they seldom explore subcultural contrasts between them. Intergroup differences are sometimes given a certain amount of attention in historically oriented works that treat waves of immigration as successive cohorts moving through poverty. Writers in the Frazier tradition are of course focusing their attention explicitly on a particular ethnic unit, Negroes. These authors devote much discussion to broad socioeconomic characteristics that actually are associated statistically with low income regardless of ethnic status. Yet they tend very much to treat these characteristics as if they were attributes of the ethnic minority without reference to other dimensions. Thus, in spite of occasional disclaimers, we find that many statements about "the Negro family" are not true of high-income Negro households but are true of a high percentage of poor non-Negro families. This amounts to representing what are really class characteristics as if they were racial or ethnic features.

Some of the social scientists most specifically interested in class subcultures as such give recognition to the existence of ethnic or national differences. At the same time, however, they emphasize that these ethnic differentials are quite minor in comparison to the commonalities within strata and the contrasts between classes. This is the view taken in Gans's work on Italian-Americans. The same point has an important place in Lewis' model. One recalls his thesis that not only his Mexican and Puerto Rican families but also lower-class groups in many parts of the world share the same poverty culture. This generalization stands in need of careful testing by full ethnographic studies, as urged in earlier sections above.

Some intriguing aspects of interrelationship among ethnicity, class, and poverty seem to emerge from another work examined earlier: Charles Keil's *Urban Blues*. It will be recalled that Keil argues strongly for the validity of a specifically ethnic subculture, a "Negro way of life." Yet, as we saw in chapter 4, pages 84–87, his subcultural inventory is actually made up largely of traits described by other authors as features of a class pattern in which ethnic variations are absent or unimportant. This contradiction is highlighted when Keil himself uses phrases such as, "the black man on the corner, like most slum dwellers everywhere . . . "[17] It is further emphasized when he cites Lewis and suggests only rather minor, tentative, relative differences between the family patterns he finds in "Negro culture" and those seen by Lewis in the "culture of poverty." In the course of his panegyric on black culture, Keil takes issue with views expressed by the novelist Ralph Ellison. Yet in the course of the very essay cited by Keil the anthropologist, Ellison the artist and critic defines—more clearly, concisely, and convincingly than any social scientist known to me—the subcultural status of Negro Americans as an ethnic subsociety. It is all summed up in two brief passages.

The American Negro people is North American in origin and has evolved under specifically American conditions: climatic, nutritional, historical, political and social. It takes its character from the experience of American slavery . . . emancipation . . . race and caste discrimination, and from living in a . . . highly mobile society possessing . . . an explicitly stated equalitarian concept of freedom. Its spiritual outlook is basically Protestant, its system of kinship is Western, its time and historical sense are American, and its secular values are those professed, ideally at least, by all of the people of the United States.

Culturally this people represents one of the many subcultures which make up that great amalgam of European and native American cultures which is the culture of the United States. This "American Negro culture" is expressed in a body of folklore, in the musical forms of the spirituals, the blues and jazz; an idiomatic version of American speech . . . a cuisine; a body of dance forms and even a dramaturgy which is generally unrecognized because still tied to the more folkish Negro churches.
. . . .

In brief, there is an American Negro idiom, a style and a way of life, but none of this is inseparable from the conditions of American society, nor from its general modes of culture—mass distribution, race and intra-national conflicts, the radio, television, its system of education, its politics. If general American values influence us, we in turn influence them—speech, concept of liberty, justice, economic distribution, international outlook, our current attitude toward colonialism, our national image of ourselves as a nation. And this despite the fact that nothing which black Americans have won as a people has been won without a struggle.[18]

Keil objects to what he calls "the melting-pot tone of Ellison's remarks" and argues that some of these remarks are valid only for "the 'black bourgeoisie' and a cluster of Negro intellectuals." The partial accuracy of this objection only reveals that Keil really is thinking more in terms of class than of ethnic status apart from class. That is to say, Keil's formulation has the effect of excluding the Negro middle class and black intellectuals from the ethnic group. A quite similar position is taken by many Black Power spokesmen and other militant advocates of Negro advancement on the grounds that mobility and success for the black man in the white man's world typically exact the price of his repudiating Negro identity and, in effect, selling out his masses of black brothers. There can be little doubt that this general analysis does go to the heart of the dilemma imposed on upward mobile Negroes by American society; it is certainly a telling political polemic; and it may yet become an ideological theme of a successful social movement. But it is not helpful when these points are allowed to obscure the problem of interrelations between class and ethnic group, as in Keil's discussion.

Nevertheless, the insights implied in this identity analysis do include a point that probably is quite significant for the problem of ethnic group and class. This is the probability that the ethnic identity and subcultural distinctness of all or many minorities are greatest for group members who are poor. Ethnic cultural contrasts may regularly decrease both with individual mobility and with improvements in group fortunes. If this is indeed true, it would help to explain why ethnic subsocieties seem to be confused with socioeconomic strata most often at the lowest status levels. Here we may also have a reason why the same confusion occurs particularly in reference to Negroes: they constitute an ethnic category with a very high proportion of low incomes. Probably the only significant minority with a higher percentage living in poverty is American Indians. The latter are outside the equation for at least two reasons: their poverty is less visible than that of Negroes, while their ethnic subculture is more obviously distinct.

The interpretation that ethnic contrasts vary with socioeconomic level also raises questions about the intersocietal applicability of Lewis' poverty culture. One implication of this interpretation would be that middle and elite strata might be expected to show greater intersocietal commonalities than the subcultures of the world's poor. This position might well be argued on other grounds as well. Indeed, one of the contradictions within Lewis' model is rather sharpened by these considerations. The provincialism and narrow horizons emphasized by Lewis in his generalizations on poverty culture might be commonalities of *form* shared by many groups of poor people. A likely consequence, however, would seem to be mutual isolation leading to retentions of mutually exotic cultural *content*. This would represent the opposite extreme from the cosmopolitan sharing by modern elites of worldwide social networks, international organizations, communications media, and transportation facilities.

On the basis of existing evidence it is not possible to resolve all outstanding issues connecting class and ethnic status. It is both possible and necessary, however, to emphasize the need for inquiry into these matters. Indeed, ethnic subcultural variety may well be a dimension no less worthy of attention in poverty research than social stratification. Perhaps we should revise the formulation offered at the outset of this section with respect to primary and secondary dimensions of differentiation. It is worth suggesting that both stratification and ethnicity be considered primary dimensions for study among the lower-class poor, both equally important for defining the framework of such research. At the very least this would mean that field work should focus upon identifiable ethnic collectivities. Thus we need ethnographies not only of the poor but of the Negro poor, the white Anglo-Saxon Protestant poor, the Irish poor, the American Indian poor, and no doubt many more.

At the same time, however, care must be taken that this approach not lead back again to one of the errors repeatedly criticized here: confounding and confusing ethnicity with class status. This confusion might be reinstated and strengthened if *all* studies of poor people were also studies of ethnic minorities. Research must also be done among poverty-stricken subsocieties that are not structured primarily in terms of ethnicity, collectivities whose members do not see themselves and are not viewed by outsiders primarily in terms of ethnic identities. In the United States this does not simply mean studying lower-class white Anglo-Saxon Protestants. (Contrary to one widespread usage, these "WASP's" are of course an ethnic category, regardless of the fact that they do not usually occupy the status of a minority.) The point is rather that we need knowledge and understanding of social situations in which ethnic boundaries do not correspond closely with lines between the poverty-stricken and the non-poor. Such situations no doubt exist in some American urban slums whose populations are heterogeneous in national origin, regional background, religious affiliation, and other indices of ethnic differentiation. If there is a subculture of poverty that is strictly associated with a socioeconomic stratum and independent of ethnic or other non-class variables, studies carried out under the conditions just described will be essential to defining that subculture. Present and future research along these lines (see Notes, page 195) is thus a necessary complement to the other approach advanced in these pages, multiple ethnographies of ethnically definable subgroups among the poor. A synthesis of findings from these various lines of inquiry will be required to produce full understanding of the cultural correlates of poverty.

CONCEPTIONS OF POVERTY SUBCULTURES AS CONSTRUCTS TO BE TESTED

This discussion has repeatedly led us to the conclusion that existing descriptions of culture patterns among the poor lack sufficient documentation to be convincing as they stand. Indeed, these portrayals consist largely of hypothetical constructions, many of which have hardly been tested against the most relevant kinds of empirical evidence. These conceptions of poverty subculture can thus be treated as descriptive models or constructs, and the kinds of information needed to test their validity can be suggested. This will be done here by recasting several models, selected from the literature, in terms of one or more major hypotheses and a series of derived or supportive propositions. Following each of these major and minor propositions from published constructs, opposing or alternative propositions will be suggested. This will give us a series of alternate predictions of what direct investigation would reveal about major aspects of the life of the poor. These pairs of predictive hypotheses will thus amount to a tentative guide to the kinds of information needed to confirm or invalidate many of the principal generalizations concerning the culture of the poor.

Three constructs have been selected for this exercise. Oscar Lewis' "culture of poverty," already discussed at length (particularly in chapter 3), is included because it is the most extensive and detailed representation of lower-class subculture. The other two formulations are also among the contributions most often cited in learned discussions of poverty and the poor. Walter Miller's "focal concerns of lower-class culture" was one of the early stimulants of contemporary interest, among both social scientists and social workers, in poverty and its connections with crime (cf. chapter 2, pp. 43–45). Herbert Gans's treatment of "subculture and class" is particularly useful for our purpose, for it draws on a wide selection of studies concerning the lower-class poor and systematically contrasts the findings of such studies with constructs of both working-class and middle-class subcultures (cf. chapter 5, pp. 110–13). The work of other authors on the lower class discussed earlier (Frazier, Glazer, Moynihan; chapter 2) is not dealt with in the present discussion. The portrayals of the poor by those writers are both too narrow in scope and too crudely conceptualized to be useful for this analysis.

The Culture of Poverty, As Conceived
by Oscar Lewis

Ruling Hypothesis 1. The culture of poverty is "a subculture of Western society with its own structure and rationale, a way of life handed down from generation to generation along family lines . . . a culture in the traditional anthropological sense that it provides human beings with a design for living, with a ready-made set of solutions for human problems."[19]

Ruling Alternative 1. The distinctive patterns of social life at the lowest income levels are determined by structural conditions of the larger society beyond the control of low-income people, not by socialization in primary groups committed to a separate cultural design. Otherwise stated, the design for living received by the poor through socialization is not significantly distinct from that of the society as a whole, but the actual conditions of low-income life are importantly inconsistent with actualization of this cultural design.

It might be argued that these two interpretations are not mutually exclusive because there is one formulation in which they could be harmonized and combined. That is, one might contend that the factors described in the alternative have operated for some time and produced a result that corresponds with the conditions described by the hypothesis. This is a historical interpretation, and in fact some such thinking is either explicit or implicit in much writing on the poor. For clarification it should therefore perhaps be stated that the hypothesis and its alternative are put forward here only as models of presently ongoing social life. They refer to the immediate sources and patterning of social behavior on the part of living generations of people who can be directly observed by the ethnographer. Historical explanations are a separate matter. Strictly speaking, contemporary ethnography alone cannot provide all the evidence that is relevant to choosing among historical interpretations. Once a choice is made between the above hypothesis and alternative on the basis of ethnographic research, then past sources of present conditions can be sought by examining historical evidence. In the meantime, however, our understanding of present systems and subsystems should not be prejudiced by premature interpretations of what we think historical trends may have produced.

Proposition 1a. Patterned lack of participation in important aspects of the wider society is an internally perpetuated characteristic of the culture of the poor: "The disengagement, the non-integration, of the poor with respect to the major institutions of society is a crucial element in the culture of poverty."[20]

Alternative 1a. Socioeconomically disadvantaged groups show strikingly differential participation in various specific institutional areas of the wider society; these contrasting patterns are imposed and perpetuated externally through institutional structures and processes, particularly recruitment avenues, that are beyond local control. More specifically, it is predicted that poor populations under study may show some of the following patterns of differential participation.

High participation: police-courts–prison complex, armed services, welfare system, primary public education.

Low participation: stable employment, property ownership, political parties, labor unions, higher education.

Proposition 1b. Knowledge of the dominant values of the wider society is contradicted by actual behavior, which is conditioned by local socialization: "People with a culture of poverty are aware of middle-class values, talk about them and even claim some of them as their own, but on the whole they do not live by them."[21]

Alternative 1b. Many common values are shared with the dominant strata or the total culture, but specialized alternative values are accepted where contradictions between cultural ideals and situational conditions are sharp for the poor. Behavior will generally be consistent with either shared values or specialized values, depending on the context. For example, it is predicted that groups of the poor under study will show adherence to some of the following specific value orientations.

Common values: education an instrumental desideratum, material comfort a desirable goal, self-sufficiency an admired mode, competition and cooperation appropriate in different contexts.

Specialized values: official authority is neither benign nor trustworthy but can be manipulated; blue-collar crime is less blameworthy than white-collar crime; conventional family life is desirable but not necessarily attainable; the wider society is basically discriminatory against the poor.

Proposition 1c. Local social structure is practically non-existent beyond the household: "When we look at the culture of poverty on the local community level, we find . . . above all a minimum of organization beyond the level of the nuclear and extended family."[22]

Alternative 1c. Low-income urban districts have describable local social structures including many groups and relationships analogous to those found in communities elsewhere in the wider society, as well as some elements that are specialized adaptations to conditions of socioeconomic disadvantage or marginality. Depending upon the particular area and population studied, it is predicted that at least some of the following elements will be found.

Analogous elements: community council, political ward organizations, denominational church congregations, law-abiding youth groups, friendship associations, personal social networks, interhousehold reciprocity, various service institutions.

Specialized elements: civil rights or minority-advancement groups, poverty-oriented social change movements, store-front churches, juvenile gangs, adult blue-collar criminal associations, other voluntary associations.

Proposition 1d. Family structure and process are unstable and disorganized: "On the family level the major traits of

the culture of poverty are the absence of [prolonged and pro-
tected] childhood . . . early initiation into sex, free unions or
consensual marriages . . . abandonment of wives and children
. . . female- or mother-centered families . . . sibling rivalry,
and competition for limited goods and maternal affection."[23]

Alternative 1d. The domestic group may frequently be un-
conventional in form and process, but both households and
kinship are organized in ways that are adaptive to externally
imposed conditions. In particular, it may be predicted that
the following elements will be found.

The conventional biparental family is widely preferred
and is the extant form for a substantial proportion of
households at any one time and through significant phases
of many individuals' life cycles.

The early socialization of children tends to be shared by
a wider group of kinsmen, other adults, and peers, rather
than being more concentrated in the nuclear family; this
may contribute to a healthy early maturity and the adaptive development of multiple affective ties and potential
sources of emotional security.

Early sexuality need not be maladaptive except in cases
of unwanted pregnancy, a circumstance partly taken care of
by somewhat flexible standards of legitimacy and potentially resolvable by knowledge of and access to contracep-
tion.

Consensual unions provide a flexible adaptation that is
functional under conditions in which fluctuating economic
circumstances, actual or threatened incarceration, and
other external conditions often make it advisable for cohab-
iting pairs to separate either temporarily or permanently
and contract alternative unions, again either temporary or
lasting.

Many family events superficially describable as desertion
or abandonment actually involve one or more of the following elements, each of which may be adaptive:

separation by mutual consent, sometimes including considerations of alternative means of support for mother and children;

informal and extralegal but effective adoption which shifts dependents to households better able to support them;

attenuated affinality, in which kin ties and support sources established through the marital union continue to function in the absence of the husband;

reunion, planned or otherwise, after temporary separation;

support of fatherless families through other lines of kinship connection.

Female-centered or mother-focused households, statistically somewhat more frequent than in other social strata, may be positively functional because of factors such as those just listed, plus others.

Husbandless mothers may seek to identify positive male models for their children among kinsmen, neighbors, or others; children themselves may also seek and find such identifications.

Identification with admired figures in peer groups may occur earlier than is typical in higher social strata.

Intrafamily competition both for goods and for affection is mitigated by the greater resources available through extended kin ties and non-kin associations.

Proposition 1e. Personal identity, character, and world view are weak, disorganized, and restricted: "On the level of the individual, major characteristics are a strong feeling of marginality, of helplessness, of dependency and of inferiority ... weak ego structure, confusion of sexual identification, lack of impulse control ... little ability to defer gratification and to plan for the future ... resignation and fatalism ... belief in male superiority ... tolerance for psychological pathology ... provincial and locally oriented ... very little sense of history."[24]

Alternative 1e. The general contours of individual cognitive and affective orientations to the world are predominantly realistic and adaptive, even assuming that these orientations are descriptively much as presented in Proposition 1e. More specifically:

Feelings of marginality, helplessness, and dependency are often in accord with the objective character of life circumstances.

Conflict about sex roles appears in the context of dramatic contradictions between dominant value ideals and objective practical possibilities, thus not requiring the depth interpretation of psychopathology.

Impulse control and gratification deferral vary situationally and may be maximized when a future reward can be realistically predicted.

Planning for the future occurs when prospective alternatives are perceived as at least potentially controllable by choice, which may be relatively infrequent.

Resignation and fatalism may readily give way to individual aspiration or group confidence when there is a change in perceived opportunities.

Assertions of male superiority reflect a value orientation of the *total* culture, with perhaps some added strength for the lower class, in the form of compensation or wishful thinking in relation to objective limits on the effectiveness of the conventional male role.

Relative tolerance for behavior conventionally regarded as pathological may be positively functional in terms of at least two aspects of socioeconomic deprivation:

Some conventionally abnormal behavior patterns are adaptive (cf. Alternative 1d).

Often the only extracommunity treatment available to disturbed individuals is punitive or custodial.

Provincialism and local orientation are balanced by knowledge or beliefs about the wider world, including historical conceptions, political orientations, and by some sense of identity with other groups of the poor.

Concerns of Lower-Class Culture, as Conceived by Walter Miller

Ruling Hypothesis 2. "The lower class way of life . . . is characterized by a set of focal concerns . . . a distinctive patterning of concerns which differs significantly, both in rank order and in weighting, from that of American middle class culture." These concerns constitute pairs of "perceived alternatives."[25]

Major Alternative 2. The concerns listed here (as well as many others) are common to the lower class and to *other strata;* but the values involved are expressed differently in one class as compared with another, both verbally and in nonverbal behavior, because the life conditions and available resources of the lower socioeconomic brackets are different from those of other groups.

Ruling Hypothesis 2a. Lower class concerns generate a distinctively high rate of delinquency and crime: "The commission of a range of illegal acts is either explicitly supported by, implicitly demanded by, or not materially inhibited by factors relating to the focal concerns of lower class culture."[26]

Major Alternative 2a. Illegal and nonnormative behavior is associated with similar value alternatives among both the poor and the non-poor; the major contrast is in the *kinds* of delinquency or norm violation committed or encouraged; the main reasons for the contrast are the same as in Major Alternative 2.

Proposition 2b. "*Trouble:* Concern over 'trouble' is a dominant feature of lower class culture . . . 'trouble' involves a distinction of critical importance for the lower-class community—that between 'law-abiding' and 'non-law-abiding' behavior."[27]

Alternative 2b. Legal trouble is important to middle-class people as well as to the poor, and the interstrata differences lie mainly in two areas directly related to the structural positions of these groups in the society as a whole:

Blue-collar crime (burglary, larceny, robbery, assault, peace disturbance, gambling, offenses associated with alcohol and drugs, etc.) as opposed to white-collar crime (embezzlement, tax evasion, offenses against rules of regulatory agencies, contract breaches, bribery, fraud, behavior leading to divorce or scandal, etc.).

Differential vulnerability to official agencies of social control: e.g., concentration of police in poverty and minority districts, lack of access by the poor to either legal or extralegal protection against the police and courts, discrimination by police and courts against the poor and racial minorities.

Proposition 2c. "*Toughness.*" This lower-class concern involves "physical prowess . . . 'masculinity' . . . and bravery in the face of physical threat."[28]

Alternative 2c. Middle-class men are also quite concerned about these male virtues. The apparent tendency for the disadvantaged to express this concern in physical terms is sufficiently explained by their lack of control over resources and power that would enable them to demonstrate their masculine toughness in the additional ways available to the more privileged: nonphysical competitiveness, ambition, ruthlessness, and authoritarianism (any of which may provoke legal sanctions if carried to a sufficient extreme). Consistent with this, it may be further predicted that achievement of relative wealth or power even within the disadvantaged community tends to exempt a man from the more directly physical requirements of toughness.

Proposition 2d. "*Smartness:* . . . the capacity to outsmart, outfox, outwit, dupe, 'take,' 'con' another or others . . . to achieve a valued entity—material goods, personal status—through a maximum use of mental agility and a minimum use of physical effort."[29]

Alternative 2d. Here again class contrasts consist of different modes that express the same values in accordance with the socioeconomic resources available but lead to different types of law breaking and norm violation. Consider "smart" businessmen, lawyers, and politicians in relation to white-collar crime, the "wise" or "hip" college student in relation to cheating and plagiarism, the systematic deceptiveness of whole professions such as advertising, or the commonplace prevarication of statesmen euphemistically referred to in terms of "credibility gaps."

Proposition 2e. "*Excitement:* . . . the search for excitement or 'thrill' . . . use of alcohol . . . gambling of all kinds . . . adventuring with sex and aggression, frequently leading to 'trouble.' "[30]

Alternative 2e. Here the analysis would parallel that in the last entry, except that in this case the privileged strata are even more able to maximize the value in question without being adjudged delinquent or criminal.

Proposition 2f. "*Fate:* . . . the concern with fate, fortune or luck. . . . Many lower class individuals feel that their lives are subject to a set of forces over which they have relatively little control."[31]

Alternative 2f. In this case, the attitude attributed to the lower class is adaptive, since the sense of lacking control over one's destiny embodies considerable realism; middle-class people tend to have similar attitudes with respect to the relatively restricted aspects of their lives over which they feel they have little control, e.g., the eventuality of nuclear warfare.

Proposition 2g. "*Autonomy* . . . has a special significance and is distinctively patterned in lower-class culture. The discrepancy between what is overtly valued and what is covertly sought is particularly striking in this area."[32] That is, ambivalence and conflict between explicit rebellion against controls or authority and covert attraction to the nurturance and dependence inherent in restrictive institutions and relationships.

Alternative 2g. Perfectly analogous conflicts are a commonplace among middle-class Americans, though for the poor the ambivalence is exacerbated by the twin factors of more arbitrary external authority against which to develop resentment and fewer restrictive but security-giving social settings outside of punitive "total institutions."[33]

Lower-Class Subculture, As Conceived by Herbert Gans

Ruling Hypothesis 3. Social classes are "strata in the larger society. . . . The strata are composed of subcultures and subsocial structures. . . . The strata are defined as subcultures on the assumption that relationships, behavior patterns, and attitudes are related parts of a social and cultural [sub] system."[34]

Major Alternative 3. Classes are primarily structural units (subsocieties) rather than cultural entities (subcultures). The major differences between classes are matters of socioeconomic and political placement within the structure of the whole society. Contrasts in relationships, behavior, and attitudes are secondary and are derived more from situational adaptation to structural placement than from contrasting socialization in distinct systems of custom and belief. (Cf. Alternative 1.)

Proposition 3a. "The lower-class subculture is distinguished by the female-based family and the marginal male. Although a [wider] family circle may also exist, it includes only female relatives. The male . . . is physically present only part of the time, and is recognized neither as a stable nor dominant member of the household."[35]

Alternative 3a. While this household form may be statistically prevalent, this does not necessarily mean that it is culturally preferred. It may be a relatively uncommon and often temporary adaptation to extrafamilial situational stresses (cf. Alternative 1*d*). Rather than a "family circle" composed entirely of females, families are commonly supported in part through a variety of kinship ties, including affinal links and involving both sexes.

Proposition 3b. "The male, whether husband or lover, . . . participates only minimally in the exchange of affection, and has little to do with the rearing of children. Should he serve as a model for the male children, he does so largely in a negative sense."[36]

Alternative 3b. This portrayal may be least accurate for those families that are more or less conventionally biparental, perhaps more often valid for households that remain female-centered for some time. For children in the latter kind of family, however, older kinsmen and other adult males may serve as positive male models.

Many more or less stably married men will be found to have close and affectionate relationships with children in their households, particularly male offspring beyond infancy. (Cf. Alternative 1*d*.)

Proposition 3c. "In the lower class, the segregation of the sexes . . . is complete. The woman tries to develop a stable routine in the midst of poverty and deprivation; the action-seeking man upsets it . . . she will try to encourage her children to seek a routine way of life."[37]

Alternative 3c. Sex roles are neither so uniform nor so mutually inconsistent and incompatible as this proposition indicates. For example, it may be predicted that:

Many individuals of both sexes practice compartmentalization of "action-seeking" and "routine-seeking" in different aspects of their lives (e.g., routine-orientation at home, action-orientation on nights out).

Many of the more stable families may include husband-fathers who are more routine-oriented than the proposition would suggest.

Some couples may maintain relatively stable, perhaps childless, unions through both partners' being action-oriented.

Some female family heads may encourage an adaptive action-seeking orientation in their children of one or both sexes.

Proposition 3d. "For lower class men, life is almost totally unpredictable. If they have sought stability at all, it has slipped from their grasp so quickly, often, and consistently that they no longer pursue it. . . . Relationships with women are of brief duration . . . there can be no identification with work at all. . . . Education is rejected. . . ."[38]

Alternative 3d. Orientations toward predictability and stability are more complex and varied than this proposition indicates. Illustrative predictions include the following.

In addition to men who have no identification with stability, there are others who desire and seek stability in some or all aspects of life, and still others who are more or less ambivalent about these concerns.

With respect to sexual and marital relationships, see Alternative *3c*.

In the realm of work, varying degrees of continuity and stability are achieved by some proportion of men in conventional low-level occupations and perhaps also in some illegal pursuits; when more desirable economic opportunities become available advantage is taken of them.

Rejection of primary education is infrequent; rejection of secondary or higher education is not universal.

For some individuals, the completion of secondary school may be rejected, not because it interferes with action-seeking, but because it promises little or no actual predictable advantage.

This series of constructs presents a substantial set of empirical questions to be answered by ethnographic research. Some relevant approaches, techniques, and kinds of data to be sought in such studies are suggested in the Appendix, pages 173–90.

6 Conclusion: Alternative Views of Poverty and the Poor, Present and Future

A number of ideas have been reviewed here, a variety of problems explored, and some suggestions offered for future research. From this discussion there emerge three broad formulations or intellectual models representing varying views of the lower class as a subsociety, its lifeways as a subculture, the sources of subcultural patterns, and associated questions of public policy looking to the future.

These three models emerge from the foregoing discussion in the sense that they are logical alternatives growing out of available knowledge about poverty, society, and culture. While these models can be said to have their roots in different schools of thought, they are not meant to represent positions taken by particular writers.

Model 1: Self-perpetuating Subsociety with a Defective, Unhealthy Subculture

a. The lower-class poor possess a distinct subculture, and in the areas of life covered by this subculture they do not share the dominant larger culture typified by the middle class.

b. The main distinctiveness of the poverty subculture is that it constitutes a disorganized, pathological, or incomplete version of major aspects of middle-class culture.

c. The poverty subculture is self-generating in the double sense that socialization perpetuates both the cultural patterns of the group and consequent individual psychosocial inadequacies blocking escape from poverty.

d. The poverty subculture must therefore be eliminated, and the poor assimilated to middle-class culture or working-class patterns, before poverty itself can be done away with.

e. These changes may occur through revolution in under-developed societies where the poor are the majority; in the West they will be brought about by directed culture change through social work, psychiatry, and education.

Model 2: Externally Oppressed Subsociety with an Imposed, Exploited Subculture

a. The lower-class poor are a structurally distinct sub-society, and their life is therefore situationally distinct from that of all other social strata.

b. Elements of pathology, distortion, and incompleteness in the life of the lower class have their source in the structure and processes of the total system, mediated by denial of cultural resources to the poor.

c. The disadvantaged position of the poor is maintained primarily by the behavior of the higher strata, acting in their own interest as they see it, to preserve their advantages by preventing a redistribution of resources.

d. The structure of the whole society must therefore be radically altered, and the necessary redistribution of resources accomplished, before poverty can be eliminated.

e. Short of a presently unforeseeable willingness of the other subsocieties to share their advantages, these changes can come about only through revolutionary accession to power by representatives of the poor.

Model 3: Heterogeneous Subsociety with Variable, Adaptive Subcultures

a. The lower-class poor possess some distinct subcultural patterns, even though they also subscribe to norms of the middle class or the total system in some of the same areas of life and are quite nondistinctive in other areas;

there is variation in each of these dimensions from one ethnic group to another.

b. The distinctive patterns of the poverty subcultures, like those of the other subsocieties, include not only pathogenic traits but also healthy and positive aspects, elements of creative adaptation to conditions of deprivation.

c. The structural position and subcultural patterns of the poor stem from historical and contemporary sources that vary from one ethnic or regional group to another but generally involve a multicausal combination of factors, often including some of those cited above in both 1c and 2c.

d. Innovation serving the interests of the lower class to an optimal degree will therefore require more or less simultaneous, mutually reinforcing changes in three areas: increases in the resources actually available to the poor; alterations of the total social structure; and changes in some subcultural patterns.

e. The most likely source for these changes is one or more social movements for cultural revitalization, drawing original strength necessarily from the poor, but succeeding only if the whole society is affected directly or indirectly.

   (1) Such a movement would reinvigorate the poor as it developed, sweeping away subcultural patterns that are merely static adjustments to deprivation.

   (2) Particularly where the poor are a numerical minority, such a movement would have to rely significantly on suasion other than physical force to achieve its wider objectives, so that revolution on the classical model would probably not be sufficient.

   (3) Social work and education, perhaps even psychiatry, might serve important secondary and supportive functions if they were reoriented in terms of the movement.

(4) The American civil rights movement is perhaps a prototype in some respects, but a successful revitalization movement serving the interests of the poor would have to be much more radical in its aims and command far greater strength.

Among the authors whose works we have reviewed here there are several whose views overlap the boundaries between these formulations. The three conceptualizations are not by any means altogether mutually exclusive. While there are many important inconsistencies between the first two, one of the intentions behind Model 3 obviously is to reconcile some of these differences by providing a framework to accommodate certain items from both of the other formulations. Thus the third model is, in part, an eclectic synthesis involving the contention that major propositions from the first two may be simultaneously valid.

At the same time, these three outlines do contain the principal theoretical themes touched upon earlier. Model 1 will be recognized as representing the dominant view in most respects. This is the case despite the fact that some of its proponents, notably Oscar Lewis, also subscribe with varying vigor to certain propositions in the other formulations. Model 1 seems to be the prevailing orientation not only among academic poverty experts but also among liberal intellectuals in general, as well as in relevant national policy-making circles. My own view of this model is that the main weight and prevailing direction of available evidence are inconsistent with it, even though most of those reporting the evidence seem to be more or less committed to this interpretation. When it is presented as a total picture of the culture of the lower class, in my considered judgment this portrayal is absurd. In this form it is little more than a middle-class intellectual rationale for blaming poverty on the poor and thus avoiding recognition of the need for radical change in our society.

It seems obvious that Model 1 constitutes the chief conceptual underpinning for dominant public policy initiatives, preeminently the "war on poverty." In this respect the influence of this conception is profoundly pernicious, unless one adopts the position that the worse relations become between the poor and the rest of society, the more likely it is that constructive change will come about. The basic message of this approach to the poor is that only after they have become conventionally respectable can they hope for a chance to leave poverty behind them. As virtually every good-sized city in the country becomes a battlefield from time to time through the 1960's, it should be apparent that this approach does not work because its intellectual foundation is a woeful distortion. The social-work solution has been given a new rationale in terms of "culture," but the policies have clearly failed and their intellectual justifications could hardly have been more thoroughly discredited.

On the other hand, none of this means that the logic of Propositions 1*a*, 1*b*, and 1*c* is inherently unreasonable or universally invalid. From a theoretical standpoint, there must be few if any cultures or subcultures with *no* dysfunctional or pathogenic elements. More concretely, there is certainly empirical evidence of pathology, incompetence, and other kinds of inadequacy among the people of the ghettos and slums, as there is in the rest of society. There can be no doubt that living in poverty has its own destructive effect on human capacities and that these impairments become part of the whole process perpetuating deprivation. The vital questions are, how important are the internal disabilities of the lower class, and how are they related to significant external factors? An incomplete but important answer seems plain already: subcultural disabilities are definitely not the whole problem and almost certainly not the principal problem. More adequate answers await research not yet done, including the kind of field work suggested earlier.

Model 2 has its roots in scholarship animated by philosophical positions of the radical left. Phrased rather broadly as it is, it is perhaps reasonably consistent with a fairly wide range on this ideological quarter, from the pessimistic orthodox Marxian view of the "lumpenproletariat" to Fanon's more optimistic vision of "the wretched of the earth." These views find no systematic or wholehearted proponents among the authors we have considered in detail. Nevertheless, the general shape of the evidence not infrequently suggests that the propositions of this model must be taken seriously. Moreover, some interpretations in our sources raise intriguing questions in this connection, such as Lewis' suggestion that poverty cultures may have been eliminated in socialist states.

In my opinion, Model 2 is another inadequate formulation, by virtue of incompleteness. That is, it covers part of the available evidence but not all of it. Nevertheless, it seems that, in a general way at least, this theory is consistent with a considerably larger part of the evidence than the first model considered. The broad structural features of Model 2 are difficult to argue against, as are its propositions on the general processes of relationship between subsocieties. The associated strategies for change are more open to question. It seems clear that stratified inequalities in both wealth and power continue to exist in societies that have undergone socialist revolutions, including some where such upheavals occurred decades ago. On the other hand, this does not necessarily mean that either poverty or lower-class subcultures persist in these societies. Again, obviously, more information is needed. On one point, however, general knowledge does seem a sufficient basis for a reasonably secure conclusion. In the United States, and perhaps in other advanced systems of mixed capitalism where the poor are distinctly in the minority, a socialist revolution by violent seizure of power in the interests of the lower class does not appear practicable.

The final model is clearly superior to the others, if it succeeds in its design. It is intended to resolve some of the major difficulties found in the present literature on poverty subcultures, as well as to synthesize the strong points of Models 1 and 2. Most of it is self-explanatory, and supporting arguments for it will be found widely scattered through this

entire essay. The predictive propositions dealing with movements for culture change follow logically from the descriptive phases of the model. Nevertheless, one could hardly consider these suggestions anything more than speculative. This
remains true partly because existing empirical information is
nowhere nearly adequate either to validate convincingly or to
discredit fully any of these abstract conceptions. What is most
needed is fresh research leading to real ethnographies of the
poor.

SCENARIOS FOR THE FUTURE

The suggested research will best achieve its aims if it is
oriented and animated by a universalistic concept of culture.
Within this conception of panhuman adaptation, each particular culture need not be viewed as an alien mode inimical
to one's own lifeways. Each way of life can be seen as a
uniquely creative and continually developing synthesis in
which human universals and group particularities are inseparable. Similarly, this view will grant a basic human worth
and dignity to all subsocieties and to each subculture. This
requires a consistent refusal to derogate any subsystem simply
because it seems to violate one's own sectional values or to
threaten one's own subgroup interests. These are requirements not easily fulfilled, as we have seen.

Anthropologists have succeeded well in living up to these
difficult requirements while working with exotic peoples in
every faraway part of the world. They also succeeded notably
with the American Indians, though it should be remembered
that this was achieved mainly after the Indians had ceased to
pose any threat to white Americans or their interests. Can we
now accomplish the same achievement with our more familiar exotics, the savage underclasses here at home—the potentially predatory nomads who wander with the seasonal cycles
of our crops, the pockets of primitive mountain folk still living by a coal-age culture, or the marauding hostile tribes on
the frontiers of our inner cities? We have not succeeded as

yet in meeting this contemporary challenge to anthropology, though some of us have made valiant attempts. These attempts by the new anthropologists like Oscar Lewis should certainly not be scorned, even if we cannot yet praise them very highly by the older standards. The present challenge of ethnography at home is a far more difficult one than yesterday's fieldwork problems. It is much more difficult here and now to preserve the necessary social distance and creative tension between ourselves and the governors, the missionaries, the purveyors of trade goods, or the labor recruiters. We are much more directly involved in the larger system, which makes it harder to achieve the necessary quality of involvement in certain of the smaller subsystems. More pointedly, we have personal and professional interests that are firmly embedded in the dominant subsociety of this system.

Yet perhaps even this need not disqualify us entirely or make our task impossible. In the old anthropology we had to loosen our intellectual and emotional ties with Western culture considerably, engaging in a sort of professional semi-alienation to achieve a kind of transcendent viewpoint. The problem of the new anthropology is to achieve sufficient intellectual and emotional independence from the middle class, and from its dominant subculture, so that we can spend substantial time actually living our whole existence with the indigenes on the other side of the tracks, within the black ghetto, or in a public housing project. As in the old pattern, some of us might even go native, slightly and temporarily, though this is certainly a relative matter and an individual problem for each ethnographer. In short, the new problems may not differ so much in kind from the old ones, even though they certainly differ in degree.

If we can really regain the art of living with the natives, it seems reasonable to hope that the rest will flow rather naturally. We should be able to learn to see the world as it is from within the alien subsociety. We should find it possible, by following out the inner logic of the exotic subculture, to discover through direct experience the similarities of the sub-system to others as well as its differences, its order as well as its disorganized facets, its strengths and virtues along with its dysfunctions and pathologies. Gradually we should become less dependent on images of our people communicated to us by outsiders such as policemen or social workers, for we shall know the people ourselves at firsthand. Eventually we will come to regard those outsiders, not as authoritative sources of information, but as objects of study, to be examined in light of our growing experience of and through the subculture. Thus we shall then be investigating relationships between our temporarily chosen subsociety and others. Ultimately we should be able to view the total system with new eyes.

If this point is ever reached, there will be further consequences. The changed vision of the new ethnographer must sooner or later include within its focus the programs of agencies dealing with the subculture, and the policies of governments that rule over the subsociety. We are so far from this point at present that it seems hardly plausible to predict in detail what this reexamination might yield in new understanding or initiative for change. Yet some broad possibilities do appear highly likely. It seems probable that the future ethnographer of the poor will have clear knowledge of what lower-class people want; he will have considerable understanding of what they are willing and able to do, to get what they want. From this viewpoint it will seem obvious that policies and programs to "eliminate poverty" have failed partly because they were designed and launched without any such knowledge or understanding. It will be clear that this lack of success is analogous to the earlier failure of colonial regimes whose knowledge of their subjects was both superficial and distorted. Another obvious conclusion will be that uniform "antipoverty" policies lacking either understanding or respect for ethnic subcultural diversity within the subsociety, based on the shallow simplification of a homogeneous "culture of poverty," could not succeed. Again the historical parallel will be clear: imperial confusion and failure stemming from stereotyped thinking about primitives and savages.

The old arguments about whether the material condition of poverty or its "culture" must be changed first will seem as futile and irrelevant as the still older debates over the question whether subject peoples could be freed before they were "civilized," "modernized," or "prepared." It will be recognized that the many discussions about whether there was anything "worth preserving" in the poverty subcultures, essentially like those other arguments about the viability of non-Western lifeways in the modern world, suffered an irrelevance born of arrogance: they failed to recognize that the answers to these questions would ultimately depend, in significant part, on the people most directly concerned; not on the rulers but on those whom they ruled. From this perspective, the whole strategy of imposing conformity to middle-class manners and codes with the proffered reward of future affluence will have the quality of another historical echo. It will seem no less bankrupt and no less corrupt than the colonial strategy of offering the material comforts of the West to the rest of the world's peoples if only they would accept Western dictates in religion, politics, and economics.

Similarly, the "social-work solution" for the dilemmas of poverty at home will stand revealed as the latter-day equivalent of Christian education and uplift for the faraway heathen, and all the other baggage of the white man's burden. What has been called "maximum feasible participation of the poor" or "working with indigenous leadership" was earlier labeled indirect rule in a different but analogous context. The earlier version, like the later one, was also presented as a civilizing force, but the older policymakers were somewhat more candid about using their appointed chiefs and designated satraps to further the interests of the governors' home constituencies. Perhaps we shall come to see how, even as segregation and discrimination were being officially "prohibited," the newer forms of apartheid and the latter-day bantustans were being established here at home: "compensatory education" as a substitute for integration, whether of races or classes; training those without jobs to do the dirty work still left over after automation; painting and patching the ghetto instead of allowing people to live decently where they choose; "self-examination" and "self-help" by the poor rather than the sharing of wealth and power by the privileged; helping the poor to build "positive identities" and lots of pride—but no prosperity or power—in their slums. Further parallels will abound. Decreeing "equal rights" and "equal opportunities" for people who do not have and are not allowed equality in anything else (e.g., achievement, power) is as empty and hypocritical as the older shibboleths of "dual development" and "separate but equal." "Voting rights" for the poor, when the candidates are chosen and the parties controlled by the rich, are no more meaningful than being a British subject or holding French citizenship is for a South Sea Islander whose homeland is economically, politically, and militarily ruled by a regime of Europeans, by Europeans, for Europeans.

It may be that thinkers of another day will look back with special interest on the spirited and sophisticated debate of the 1960's between the proponents of the "services strategy" and those who favored "income strategies" in the "war against poverty." Like most activities to which the middle class attached real importance and value (seeing them as affecting their own interests), the poor did not play much part in this, even under the doctrine of maximum feasible participation. Nevertheless, it involved a lively division between those who favored winning the war with a lot of social services for the poverty-stricken few, and others who preferred victory by the weapon of a little money for everyone. The income strategists accused their opponents of advocating outmoded approaches that would merely perpetuate the problem by reinforcing the "dependency" universally considered a prime feature of poverty culture. A few even suggested that perhaps some social-service warriors enjoyed fighting poverty (and being depended on), with the implication that subtle motives might therefore prolong the war. The pro-income forces laid great stress on the importance of independence, healthy masculine economic roles, and the therapeutic effect their strategy would have on the sordid sexuality and brutish home life known by all to characterize the depraved lower class.

Moreover, they showed that these benefits would be a bargain for the whole society at only a few billion dollars per year. According to one widely publicized plan, healthy male identities and stable families would flower from Harlem to the Delta if every child in the nation were supported in the style to which public assistance recipients have become accustomed in Mississippi. A handful of reactionaries argued that such income strategies would have bad effects on the incentive to work. This carried little weight, however, for liberals and sophisticates knew that the poor had no motivation anyway, and they had other programs to take care of that problem. So the doctrine of income supports, or "transfer payments," gained supporters from the right as well as the left. Indeed, within a few years even what had previously been generally regarded as a crackpot scheme, the "guaranteed annual income," came to be discussed by congressmen. Perhaps this was partly accountable by the fact that the level of support proposed amounted to guaranteed poverty. Presumably, to some, good morals and healthy home life among the poor began to seem cheap at this price.

Although our future scholars might thus find it easy to discern absurdities by hindsight, it seems just possible that they may discern something more important in these income plans and in the general disposition of the 1960's to seek some scheme for minimal relief to the poor. It is possible that these accumulating crumbs may add up to something that those dispensing them are not bargaining for at all. Again there may be a valid analogy with the cumulative effect of minor concessions granted by the colonialists to their subjects in the mistaken belief that token acquiescences would keep the empire secure. It has been widely true that the most severely oppressed peoples and subsocieties have seldom rebelled or risen up effectively. Yet even slight improvements in the level of life and hope have often liberated quite unsuspected strengths, and rising hopes have led, not just to frustration, but to creative forms of action for change. These are commonalities in the history of many revitalization movements, some of which have succeeded in overthrowing old orders and creating new ways of life.

Possibly something like this may be what the confused struggles of the 1960's portend for the poor in America and elsewhere. We must hope that a new anthropology will soon be able to tell us whether this is the case and if so, something about what form it may be expected to take. We must hope also that the beginning of a coming confrontation between the poor and the rest of society has not already so angered and embittered crucial groups that no ethnographer can study them. There is a tragic possibility that the issue is already joined, on battlefields ranging from exploding ghettos to bullet-scarred land claims in the mountains and deserts of the Southwest or to the violently disputed fishing grounds of Pacific Northwest rivers. Our nation, and through its dominion the Western world as a whole, seems little prepared to meet the foreseeable revitalization of the poor with anything other than the reflexes of the cop on the beat in the ghetto, the posse in National Guard uniforms, and the world policeman. Perhaps there will be no new anthropology, no creative resynthesis by the oppressed, but only another long night of blood and pain.

Postscript: A Proposal for Empowering the Poor To Reduce Inequality

BACKGROUND

The proposal outlined in the following pages springs from the same concerns and is shaped by the same framework of thought as the rest of this book. Yet the plan suggested here goes well beyond the central purposes of the book. Those purposes were to evaluate existing interpretations of poverty; to probe the implications for social policies; and to propose measures for improving our knowledge and understanding of the poor. This may lead to more effective policies in the future. It is all too obvious, however, that our society needs new ways of dealing with the problems of poverty now—not merely at some future point to be determined by progress in research. This postscript proposes a way of meeting this immediate need.

This proposal reflects the urgency of dealing with the national crisis of poverty and related forms of social disadvantage. Such plans must not proceed from any illusion that present knowledge provides a clear guide to foolproof measures. On the contrary, social planners must originate fresh initiatives for change even as they recognize that existing knowledge is extremely imperfect. This will certainly deprive us of any confidence that total answers or certain solutions are at hand. At the same time, however, this recognition should also free us from the limitations of using presently accepted theories of poverty as the only bases for action. One reasonable response to the inadequacy of widely accepted interpretations of poverty is to propose action programs based on alternative interpretations.

A major source of the need for new solutions is the demonstrated failure of existing antipoverty programs and the predictable failure of additional approaches now on the horizon. It is widely agreed that the traditional programs of the welfare establishment have proved inadequate. A principal reason for this is that these programs have not enabled the poor to act in behalf of their own interests, either individually or collectively. Indeed, conventional welfare approaches have often had the opposite effect of perpetuating and reinforcing the dependency and powerlessness of the poor.

The "war on poverty" of the last few years was supposedly designed to overcome these very deficiencies in older approaches. It has neither accomplished this aim nor shown much promise that it will do so. The recent federal antipoverty effort has contributed substantial new resources to old-line social service and welfare agencies. Federal help has typically not required any basic change in agency policies, and thus in effect it has reinforced their traditional orientation. Moreover, it is generally true across the country at the local level, where antipoverty programs are actually carried out, that control over policy lines and action decisions has changed little. By and large this control is firmly held by the traditional power centers of municipalities, counties, and states. This remains true despite the myths of federal intervention and the ornaments of token "participation by the poor."

This means that there has been no significant increase in the power of poor people to act in behalf of their own interests. Under these conditions, there is little or no reason to expect that results from the newer combinations of services, training programs, and "community action" projects will be much different from the older ones. It is equally discouraging that the "war on poverty" is mainly aimed at changing the "culture of poverty" rather than altering the condition of being poor. Not only are the culture patterns of the poor very imperfectly understood, but it is highly doubtful that any "culture of poverty" is the main force perpetuating socioeconomic inequality. As long as the "war on poverty" is focused mainly on changing the supposed customs and values of the poor—rather than on altering the economic and political structure of the nation—it will have little effect on poverty.

The main ideas presently being widely discussed, tried out experimentally here and there, and possibly scheduled for national implementation within the forseeable future are various forms of direct income support for the poor: guaranteed annual income, negative income tax, family allowances. The main contribution of these programs would be to establish an absolute minimum below which no family's or unattached individual's disposable income could fall. Such an approach can be expected to fail because it is based on a misunderstanding of the poverty problem in an affluent society with an ideology of equality. The segments of the poor and their partisans or supporters who are in motion today, creating a national crisis by their outbursts of protest, are not demanding some absolute minimal level of economic security. On the contrary, they are demanding equality—if not total equalization then radically greater equality. This demand applies not merely to economic welfare but to all the material and psychic benefits of membership in our society. This is not to say that a minimum livelihood should not be vouchsafed to all; nor is it implied that this security would not be welcomed by many among the poor. The point is that no measures of minimal income support, whether presented as welfare payments or as guaranteed subsistence, can solve the basic problem of inequality.

With all this in mind, the proposal put forward here is consistent with Model 3, outlined in chapter 6 above, portraying the poor as a heterogeneous subsociety with variable subcultures. The key to this proposal is to place substantial new economic, social, and political resources under the control of the poor so that they will have the power to act in such a way as to reduce their inequality significantly. Reducing inequality does not mean what has come to be called "equal opportunity." It means equitability of results in the sense of achievement, fulfillment, and enjoyment of the rewards and satisfactions already generally available to citizens outside disadvantaged groups.

THE NEED

It has long been a cherished belief in this country that the poor should overcome poverty themselves. We now know that under modern conditions this has proved impossible for about one quarter of our citizens. Because of historically developed inequalities, equal rights today do not bring about genuinely equal opportunity for these people. Laws that guarantee equal rights cannot create actual equality for those who control only the most inadequate economic, educational, and political resources. We are all paying for this failure of our society. The cruel loss of lives and property in our burning cities makes it imperative that we find new responses to unemployment and powerlessness among the poor. In order to deal with these problems effectively, we must transcend the principle of guaranteed equality even though this principle itself is only barely established in national life. It is necessary to move on immediately to special rights and positive discrimination in favor of the human groups heretofore most disadvantaged.

The program suggested here does not deal with all aspects of poverty. No doubt comprehensive programs will be proposed by others in fields of current interest such as family structure and community organization. The present proposal is focused on the immediate and long-range economic problems of the unemployed, the underemployed, and the unskilled poor. To deal effectively with these problems it is necessary that the program cover the fields of employment and economically valuable training, as well as the related phenomenon of the powerlessness of the poor.

There are three principal reasons for choosing this focus.

One is the belief that solutions in the economic realm are both urgent in the sense of great immediate need, and fundamental in the sense that little else seems possible without substantial progress in this area. Second is the hope that a concrete and radical plan in the field of employment may have an immediate appeal to people who suffer economic deprivation every day and who can readily perceive connections between employment difficulties and some of their other problems.

In the third place, germs of a radically new approach already exist in certain employment proposals that have come in the past from civil rights organizations and related sources. One of these germs is the principle of compensatory hiring articulated by Whitney Young of the Urban League. Another is the demand sometimes made by the movement for Negro advancement, that employers who claim qualified workers cannot be found, should hire people whom they consider unqualified and give them the necessary qualifications through on-the-job training.

These ideas clearly go beyond the formulas of equal rights and equal opportunities. The common principal underlying them is that after centuries of severe denial of opportunity the victims of this deprivation cannot possibly catch up through merely equal opportunity. Carried to their logical conclusion, these ideas lead to the demand for a comprehensive national program of positive discrimination in favor of the presently underprivileged. Bayard Rustin has recently pointed out that to win World War II we effectively employed huge numbers of workers without standard qualifications. We must do the same on a larger scale, and with more imagination, to avoid losing today's war of the cities.

THE PROGRAM

Employment

The heart of this proposal is a national commitment to positive discrimination in employment. Present patterns and past trends of employment and job advancement, as reflected in group unemployment rates and median family income, must be reversed to the positive advantage of the unemployed and the poor. The program should cover as many employers as possible, certainly including government agencies at all levels, extending to public utilities under government regulation and private businesses holding government contracts, and ideally encompassing educational institutions receiving government aid and all other employers engaged in interstate commerce.

The ruling consideration should be that all individuals who are unemployed or earn less than an adequate yearly income must be given realistic good-faith opportunities for employment or advancement as soon as possible. This will mean that job opportunities must frequently be opened up regardless of applicants' existing qualifications as traditionally defined. The emphasis should be on full-time work, and all employment under the program should carry reasonable hope of both permanence and advancement. The jobs to be produced should pay no less than an adequate family income for workers who are household heads, and no less than the national minimum wage or union rates, whichever is higher, for other employees.

Hiring under such a program would have to be in accordance with group priorities. The highest priority would be assigned to heads of households who are members of the nonwhite ethnic group which has the highest rate of unemployment in each local area. In practice this would mean that adult Negro males would receive first preference in most but not all areas. The remainder of the priority system could be defined in terms of the measurable relative deprivation of each significant ethnic group in each local area, including of course poor unemployed whites.

An important key to administration of the priority system would be that whenever employers claimed they could not find qualified high-priority applicants for entering positions, they should be required and enabled to establish on-the-job training for such positions. While it should be the responsi-

bility of each employer to find and recruit high-priority applicants for all job openings, a file of such applicants could be
maintained by the administering agency for the use of employers in each local area.

Training

A fundamental enabling principle of this program should
be that present policies of access and admission to institutions
and programs of training leading to employment must be
changed to give first priority to the unemployed and the poor.
This principal should be extended to all apprenticeship programs, schools, and institutions of higher learning that receive
public funds or are subject to government regulations. These
sources of economically valuable training should be required
and enabled to certify that some substantial proportion, perhaps 25 per cent, of their openings have been reserved and
offered in good faith to unemployed or poor persons.

Group priorities for admission within this quota should be
much the same as those suggested for employment, with the
significant exception that special consideration might be given
to the qualification of youth instead of the responsibility of being a household head. Some institutions of technical or higher
education might not be able to find sufficient high-priority
applicants because of the levels of skill required for entrance.
The requirement for such institutions should be that they contribute some substantial proportion of their resources, perhaps 10 per cent, in any combination of budget, personnel or
facilities, to other institutions that do offer training leading to
the necessary entrance skills.

The aim of training under this program should be not just
minimum salable skills but the highest practical level of economically valuable qualifications, for each individual en-
rolled. Sources of training should further be required to maintain close contact with employers and to adopt the basic
principle that no enrolee's training is completed until he is
employed at a level consistent with the training received. All

such training should be free to unemployed and poor persons in accordance with the provisions under finance below, and necessary living expenses should also be provided for these enrolees.

Administration

This must be a national program, requiring a considerable degree of central coordination. Yet at the same time it must be responsive to the local needs of its beneficiaries, with real power rather than token participation guaranteed for the unemployed and the poor. Probably national coordination should be carried out by an independent executive agency of the federal government with clear-cut responsibilities and definite limitations upon its power. Certainly this national office should guarantee that all provisions in the legislative charter of the program are carried out in each local area. Perhaps it should also be responsible for defining the boundaries of regional and local areas, for determining categories of staff employment and levels of staff remuneration, and for developing broad criteria of compliance to be applied to employers and training sources.

Probably the national office should supply information and advisory material which local administering agencies might use to effect cooperation and coordination among local areas. It is most important, however, that all other policy decisions, including the option of following national or regional guidelines for inter-area cooperation, should be reserved to the local administering agencies.

It might be desirable to establish regional coordinating offices with responsibilities and limitations at the regional level analogous to those of the national office. If so, such regional offices should be established on the basis of functional units, such as areas of economic geography rather than political subdivisions such as states or territories.

The local units, where most of the actual operations of the program would be carried on, would be metropolitan areas or functional rural areas, regardless of political subdivision boundaries. The administration of each local unit should be fully controlled by a board of overseers. It is most important that a predominant majority of this board be unemployed or other poor persons who are elected by their socioeconomic peers. To provide minimum insurance that real power can be held by this portion of the population, it will probably be necessary to specify that at least two thirds of the board have these qualifications and be chosen in this way.

In elections to the board, the franchise as well as the privilege of candidacy should be limited to the poor. Terms of office should be of substantial length, perhaps three or four years, and board members should probably not be allowed to succeed themselves. Membership on a local board should be understood as a full-time position, paid at no less than the minimum rates suggested earlier under employment.

To complete this structure, state and local governments, private employers, labor unions, churches, welfare agencies, and perhaps other bona fide local groups should be encouraged to nominate representatives who would make up a minority, preferably no more than one third, of the local board. Each such appointed representative would have a vote equal to that of an elected member. The terms of office and rules of succession should probably be the same for both classes of board members.

Each local unit would of course require a staff of professionals and office personnel who would work under the supervision of the local board. This staff would register and record necessary information on employers, training sources, and unemployed or poor residents within the local area. In order to carry out the provisions of the program each local staff would need to provide some equivalent of an employment placement service, a training placement service, a public works division, a complaint bureau, an investigation department, a legal aid division, and a financial grant service.

Within the nationally established staff categories already mentioned and the financial limits stipulated below, local boards should control the hiring, advancement, and replacement of local staff. This provision should perhaps be accompanied by an understanding that the national and regional offices would assist and advise in matters of staffing, especially in the initial organization of any local office.

Enforcement

In order that this program achieve its purposes, it would clearly be necessary that it have the force of law. Moreover, at least the initial procedures for enforcement would have to be in the hands of local boards. Specifically, it should be one of the major responsibilities of local boards to decide whether employers and training institutions are in compliance with the program. It should also be within the power of local boards to grant temporary exemptions from the requirements of the program to employers who can convince the board that placing high priority applicants in certain technical or advanced openings would seriously impair the business or other establishment.

Preliminary findings on these matters should be made by the local board on the basis of the records mentioned earlier under administration, additional staff investigation wherever necessary, and/or complaints registered by any resident of the local area. If the preliminary finding is one of significant failure to comply, the local board should then hold public hearings at which all interested parties would have the right to testify. Following these steps, the final judgment of the board should be issued as a public report. Upon a judgment of failure to comply, the local board should have the power to order mandatory compliance.

Appeals against orders or judgments by local boards should be to the U.S. Court of Appeals which has jurisdiction over the local area in question, with further appeals to the U.S. Supreme Court by normal legal procedure. Of course, any party to the original dispute would have the right to initiate such an appeal. Unemployed and other poor residents of the area should be entitled to all necessary council and other assistance from the local legal aid division mentioned earlier, for the purpose of pressing such an appeal.

Finance

This program would obviously require massive financing. The major direct expenditures must clearly come from the federal treasury, but control over the local application of funds should be in the hands of local boards in order that the formal power of these bodies should be given substance. One way to accomplish this result would be that all funds appropriated for the program be centrally budgeted by the national office in strict accordance with the following provisions. The finances required to run the national and regional offices could be set as a fixed, small proportion of the total appropriation. All remaining funds would then be disbursed to local units on an equal basis pro-rated according to the number of unemployed and poor residents registered in each area.

Apart from the expenses of running local offices and paying local staffs, several forms of major expenditures from these disbursed funds can be anticipated. One would be public works projects administered at the local level but perhaps subject to advisory coordination at higher levels and cooperative agreements among neighboring local boards. Another might be grants to employers who can satisfy the local board that temporary aid would enable them to make new high-priority employees a permanent part of their work force in accordance with previous provisions. Other grants might be awarded to employers to establish or expand on-the-job training, or to training institutions which would thereby increase their ability to contribute to the program. Finally, grants should certainly be available to unemployed and other poor individuals to enable them to receive training and for living expenses during training.

New Departures

Some lessons from the successes and failures of civil rights legislation may be applied here. The program must be in a genuinely binding sense compulsory for employers. The time has passed when pledges, promises, assurances of sincere good intentions, and other forms of "voluntary" program have any relevance to the problems at hand. Existing conciliation operations, such as the U.S. Community Relations Service, may continue to have positive functions in helping to arrange compliance with a program of this kind. The basic thrust of the new program itself, however, must be compulsory.

The new approach should begin by bringing the most disadvantaged and least qualified directly into a meaningful and rewarding relationship with the real world of employment and remuneration outside the slum. It is no longer enough to encourage a trickle into the job market of those deemed most nearly "ready" for a dignified and satisfying role in our society. No expansion of social welfare services for slum dwellers will accomplish what is needed. It is not sufficient to isolate groups of poor people in work centers or camps for a while in the hope that this educational experience will somehow fit them for a life with which they have had no contact. Nor will compensatory education in the public schools produce what is needed.

The wider society must now go beyond all these forms of segregation, no matter how well-intentioned they may have been. The time has come when the affluent society must admit these victims fully, freely, and directly to its own processes and institutions of self-realization. Furthermore, privileged society must be prepared for the probability that these newcomers from another life will at first often fail to function according to the standards of their new social milieu. Those who are at home in this milieu must find the necessary flexibility to make sure that the rewards of the affluent society are vouchsafed to the newcomers regardless of such initial difficulties.

Beyond this, those who are presently destitute and despairing must have a decisive voice, not some token participation, in running the projected program. While this may lead to errors and failures in administration, it is nevertheless essential to mobilize the necessary commitment of those who must be primarily responsible for the program if they are also to be its real beneficiaries.

The basic operating principles of the approach must be clear-cut, straightforward, and simple in essence. That is, the most essential criteria for administrative and policy decisions should be built into the charter of the program. This will be a safeguard against manipulation by powerful forces in the community whose interests may be inconsistent with those of the program's intended beneficiaries. This will also provide an answer to fears of mismanagement by the poor and inexperienced.

Past Precedents

While present federal programs do not begin to have the scope that is needed, there are precedents for assumption of national responsibility in employment and training. These include the 1946 Employment Act, the 1961 Area Redevelopment Act, the 1962 Manpower Development and Training Act, the 1963 Vocational Education Act, and the Economic Opportunity (Anti-Poverty) Act of 1964, as well as the Civil Rights Act of 1964. Some useful experience is no doubt available from the past operations of existing programs in vocational education and on-the-job training. However, a new plan must insure that the principles of positive discrimination and predominant local power for the poor are basic to any such programs.

It may be that in essence the present proposals resemble the maximum accomplishments that might have been hoped for from the Economic Opportunity Act when this legislation was at a formative stage or possibly even when it was awaiting implementation. Thus the ideas presented here may not be so far beyond the bounds of recent political thought in Washington as one might conclude from the present organization and operations of the "War Against Poverty." To put it another way, the present proposal may call for little more than the logical next steps required to actualize some of the more far-reaching potentialities that arose during the debate that surrounded the launching of the federal anti-poverty effort.

On the other hand, the evidence from several years of operations by this federal program make it very clear that the Office of Economic Opportunity, and especially its municipal client bureaucracies, are far from basing their operations on the principles of compulsory positive discrimination and real power for the poor. It therefore seems likely that it would be necessary to demand a new national agency to oversee and coordinate the program projected here.

ECONOMIC IMPLICATIONS

While little can be said here as to the implications of the suggested program for wider economic policy, several points should perhaps be made explicit. First, these proposals would probably require substantial diversion of federal expenditures away from current programs, no doubt including military expenditures. Second, success would depend in part on imaginative redefinition of useful roles and careers for categories of the poor presently regarded as unemployable, including older people, ADC recipients, and many unskilled individuals. Third, the program should be geared not merely to present needs but also to the predictable expansion of the employment problem due to the growing effects of automation. Fourth, implementation of these proposals could probably be expected to have an inflationary effect on the economy as a whole, and this suggests that our society is in dire need of better devices for controlling inflation than a permanent backlog of unemployment.

This brings us to the crux of the relationship between the economic difficulties of the poor and the interests of the whole society, namely the problem of full employment. It should be clear that the present proposals are not addressed directly to this broader problem. The immediate effect of the program suggested here would be to strengthen the poor, and particu-

larly the minority poor, in the existing competition for scarce
employment opportunities. If other elements in the population thereby come to feel that they too have a stake in the
overall scarcity of jobs, it may not be unrealistic to hope
that a more broadly based demand for full employment
may arise.

MUNICIPAL POSSIBILITIES

As indicated earlier, the proposed national program as a
whole is feasible only on a basis of federal legislation and
federal financing. At the same time, it is possible that local
initiatives might establish the principles of this program at
the level of municipal government.

There are several potential weaknesses and possible dangers
in such an approach which should be recognized and guarded
against. Most important, there are many reasons, including
the experience of the first years of the "War Against Poverty,"
for believing that resistance to granting genuine power to the
poor is even more determined at the municipal level than
elsewhere in the political establishment. Most large cities already have both municipal bodies and federal "anti-poverty"
agencies which are supposed to provide economic opportunities for ethnic minorities and for the poor. Perhaps the most
important single reason why these agencies have failed to
solve the problems of poverty is that the poor have no power
to make the agencies work in their interests. Any municipal
program which follows this established pattern will fail for
the same reason.

The other major danger lies in the wide-spread proclivity
of city governments and semi-official metropolitan bodies to
establish campaigns and programs for voluntary changes in the
practices of employers and training institutions. Most cities
have had such voluntary programs for some years now, and
most major employers have pledged their cooperation in programs of this kind from the federal government to city hall.
One reason among many why these projects have had little or

no effect on poverty is that they are in no sense enforceable. It may be said that a city government is in an inherently weak position to establish a compulsory program of very broad scope. Nevertheless, it must be recognized that more campaigns for voluntary change can be expected to fail just as present and earlier ones have failed.

Perhaps the basic proposition in a municipal context might be a demand that city government do its utmost to establish a local microcosm of the national design already described, or a local foundation upon which a future national program might arise. To begin with, it should be proposed that municipal government establish the employment requirements described above in relation to all possible categories of employers. The latter would certainly include all departments of city government and should be extended to contractors receiving city funds as well as firms licensed or otherwise regulated by the city. Similarly, municipal governments should be challenged to establish the training program set forth earlier in relation to all institutions under municipal control or financed or regulated in any degree by the city.

It would be essential to institute a local board of overseers as close to the national model as possible, either for the city as a local area or possibly for a metropolitan area by agreement among relevant municipalities. It should probably be underlined that control over the program, including funds appropriated for it, must be held by an elected board with a large majority of poor members. No program under the direction of an appointed municipal officer or body should be accepted as a substitute for what is needed.

Enforcement procedures paralleling those in the national design would be required, except perhaps that appeals from decisions by the board of overseers might be to the appropriate city courts. Maximum possible financial support from the city treasury would be necessary.

Recognizing that this source of funds might be limited, however, vigorous initiatives along at least two other lines might be desirable. One of these would be to explore all possibilities for increasing support from tax revenue, the other to apply for financial aid from private foundations, state governments and the federal government.

It does not appear likely that many municipal governments would readily accept such a program without massive public pressure. It is even less likely, however, that the problems of urban poverty will be significantly mitigated by a program with less ambitious purposes. The question that remains is whether any local groups that are in a position to influence municipal governments will face this challenge and meet it.

NEED FOR PUBLIC SUPPORT

Above all, no plan resembling the proposal set forth here will ever be more than an exercise in utopian theory unless it is supported by highly organized and extremely urgent mass public pressure. Indeed one suspects that the arduous struggles required to establish the principle of equal opportunity are but a prelude to the efforts required to move on to positive discrimination.

Clearly, practical results of this kind in the real world cannot be anticipated, even with great optimism, unless some such program is adopted or developed independently by an organizational force of substantial strength. Ideas of this kind must be refined by a group process leading to organizational commitment, converted into messages that can be effectively communicated to a receptive public, if such there be, and otherwise translated from a mere blueprint for change into a genuine instrument for mass public action leading to workable social innovations.

In practical political terms, the goal must be enactment of the necessary program into law by Congress. It may well be said that this is a utopian goal. Urgent public issues sometimes require and bring to reality what had seemed to be visionary theoretical solutions. The precedents of recent national legislation in civil rights and related fields show that there is potential for seemingly improbable political responses to massive and urgent public pressure. In support of the necessary program one can visualize coalitions of civil rights groups with other progressive and reformist elements, reaching the as yet largely unorganized and inarticulate poor. The result might be that very great previously wasted or destructive human energies would be liberated in a regenerative movement of potentially transcendent importance for the whole society. To compare this potentiality with what has actually been taking place in our cities, since the first insurrection in Watts, brings home the need for a bold new approach.

Appendix: Toward an Ethnographic
Research Design

CHOOSING AND DEFINING UNITS OF STUDY

The subculture constructs presented in chapter 5 (pp. 127–40) are only partial and suggestive. Nevertheless, they do represent some of the main theoretical guidelines available for research on the culture of the poor. The scope of these constructs makes it clear that to test their many constituent hypotheses would require fully rounded ethnographic studies. Accordingly, we may now consider the kinds of data needed and the research techniques appropriate for putting these models to empirical test.

In itself, the presentation of alternative hypotheses for empirical test through field work does not by any means adequately suggest what an ethnographic research project is designed to accomplish. Indeed, an ethnographic proposal framed in these terms alone would be a distortion, for it would indicate a purely deductive research design. This would omit the equally important inductive side of ethnographic methodology. No matter what principles of theory the ethnographer takes into the field, his method includes one cardinal rule. That is, he seeks to describe the specific cultural world under study by following its own internal order and logic.

Inquiries and observations in ethnography, as in other kinds of research, are necessarily limited and selective. One hallmark of ethnographic investigation, however, is that the limits and criteria of selective inquiry are not fully set prior to going into the field. On the contrary, the ethnographer must be prepared to make many decisions about lines of inquiry and methods of approach, as his data accumulate and the contours of social existence begin to unfold before him. Anthropology is quite cognizant of the basic scientific requirement that hypotheses and abstractions must be shown to conform to concrete evidence. Yet ethnography is not basically an experimental approach to particular questions, restricted by narrow requirements of precision in prediction and control. Rather, it is essentially an exploratory enterprise seeking to chart extensive unknowns.

Even the most unfettered exploratory search for a natural order must begin with some preliminary delineation of the boundaries within which the study will be carried out. As we had occasion to note earlier, this poses a basic and difficult problem for the student of lower-class life who must become an urban anthropologist. Particularly in contrast with the tribal systems which he has tended to visualize (perhaps not always accurately) as compact and neatly structured, the urban scene is bound to strike the anthropologist as being both exceedingly amorphous and inordinately complex. However, J. Clyde Mitchell is probably correct when he diagnoses this difficulty in the following terms.

> The apparent complexity of social phenomena frequently bespeaks a lack of theoretical concepts available for their analysis. . . . It is possible that the apparent complexity of social phenomena in African urban areas is due simply to the fact that we do not as yet have the perspective with which to view these phenomena and bring them into focus. This perspective can come only when we have both the accumulation of data on urban populations and analytical effort applied to these to produce the simplification which is the characteristic of good theory.[1]

In any case the problem will not be resolved simply by retrenching on the theoretical front and retreating to small, seemingly manageable units of study such as the family or household. If my contention is correct—that full ethnography is one approach that is required—then lower-class urban social settings in which this can be done must be identified and studied.

Numerous students of the urban scene, including Oscar Lewis, have either stated or implied their conviction that poor people living in cities cannot be studied by focusing on neighborhoods, localities, wards, or other sizable social units within the urban complex. This contention has not been convincingly supported, and it rests mainly on an undemonstrated assumption. This is the assertion that lower-class neighborhoods entirely lack the social structure and other defining characteristics commonly associated with the concept of community. This assumption not only begs the question but effectively precludes further investigation. This might escape notice were it not for the fact that within the very writings making these assertions one finds evidence of social units that the poor seem to regard as communities, even if the social scientists do not. These include the *vecindades* of Lewis' Mexican studies and the slum in San Juan, Puerto Rico, that he calls La Esmeralda.

The neighborhoods and districts of the poor in our cities should be studied as much to discover whether they do have a community structure, as to record any other culture patterns that may be found there. One might well begin with the very *vecindades* and slum neighborhoods described by Lewis, for despite all his abstract disclaimers he has reported a good deal of concrete information which makes it appear that these districts would repay study on the working hypothesis that they constitute local communities in some sense. Consider Casa Grande in Mexico City with its population of 700, most of whom had lived there from 15 to 30 years when Lewis worked among them, where a third of the households are united by blood ties and another fourth by other kinship bonds; where "the young people . . . belong to the same gangs, form lifelong friendships, attend the same schools, meet at the same dances held in the courtyards, and frequently marry within the *vecindad*"; where "groups of neighbors

organize raffles . . . participate in religious pilgrimages together . . . celebrate the festivals of the *vecindad* patron saints
. . . as well as other holidays"; and where, finally, "the sense
of community is quite strong."[2] We may also recall the
description, quoted earlier (chapter 3, p. 55), of La Esmeralda in San Juan with its 3600 inhabitants, its clear
physical and social boundaries, its traditional history, its political structure, its series of local institutions, and the author's
statement that it "forms a little community of its own."[3]
Many an ethnographer has, of course, had far less indication
of community structure than this when he set out to discover
evidence of social and cultural order in the life of a human
population.

Casa Grande and La Esmeralda are named collectivities
whose very linguistic designation indicates that they are conceived of as social units within the culture of their inhabitants.
It does not require more than informal and unsystematic
acquaintance with the poorer areas of typical American
cities, ranging from Philadelphia to St. Louis to Seattle (to cite
three of which I have some knowledge), to be aware of apparently similar named lower-class neighborhoods inhabited
by the poor. Assuming careful preliminary investigation and
a judicious choice of area, a skillful ethnographer could surely
settle down in such an urban section and determine what
social structure and patterns are discoverable in the lives of
its inhabitants. Whatever the outcome, such an attempt is
certainly well worth making. The dimensions, perimeters, and
other structural characteristics of social existence, indeed
much of the cultural content of the people's lives, might turn
out to be quite inconsistent with initial expectations; but this
is a commonplace in ethnography. Even if it should emerge
that the ethnographic approach will not succeed in such a
setting, this in itself would be a significant result, deserving
careful study for its own lessons.

This brings us back to the point made earlier, that units of
study and boundaries of inquiry should not be rigidly defined

before research is undertaken in the field. It is the business of ethnography to discover the shape and limits of social systems and cultural worlds. In the ethnographic process, these discoveries unfold gradually as field work proceeds, rather than their perimeters being set in advance. What look at first like urban neighborhoods may turn out to have little significance. Overlapping social units of quite different nature, networks or chains of relationships extending along many different dimensions, or a host of other structural perspectives may be much more important. Well-rounded ethnography is one good way to find out. This approach to the problem of units for study is a small-scale reflection at one level of the broad orientation urged throughout this essay. What is needed at all levels is open-ended inquiry into the nature of the cultural worlds inhabited by the poor, as free as possible of preformed definitions of our subject.

An Outline of Subcultural Materials

Even assuming the theoretical guidelines suggested earlier and working with some such tentative unit of study as that just described, many of the specific topics, emphases, and orientations of an urban ethnographic research project would undoubtedly emerge in the course of field work. Nevertheless, the interests and problems to which we have given attention thus far do suggest a minimal outline of relevant ethnographic materials. Such an outline of topics and problem areas may prove useful as a kind of checklist for urban ethnographic studies which aim to delineate local forms of subsocieties and subcultures. This particular list was drawn up with the urban lower-class poor in America as a whole in mind. Because it is intended to cover many of the major dimensions of culture considered as a universal phenomenon, however, it might not require very great revision to be useful in comparable studies of other social strata or segments. Ethnic subcultural peculiarities are clearly among the variables to consider in employing an outline such as this and in making additions as necessary for any particular piece of research. A number of much more comprehensive topical guides for ethnographic field workers have been published; obviously the suggestions offered here are not intended to replace those volumes.

1. *Habitat*
   a. Metropolitan setting
   b. Area boundaries
   c. Natural features, flora, fauna
   d. Land use
   e. Physical structures
2. *Demography*
   a. Population size
   b. Racial composition
   c. Spatial distribution
   d. Sex and age distributions
   e. Rates of birth, mortality, morbidity
   f. Density and mobility
3. *Economics*
   a. Basic economic units: individuals; households; kin groups; institutional groups, quasi-groups.
   b. Resources and utilization: sources and levels of income, prices, consumption, credit, savings, property, housing, rents; social and political "capital"; changes in all these.
   c. Work and employment: occupations; unemployment; skills; sex and age dimensions; recruitment; stability.
   d. Community economic institutions: commercial establishments; services; economic crime.
   e. Extracommunity economic influences: places of work; income from or support to distant kinsmen and others; buying or selling outside the area; governmental influences; communications media.
4. *Social Structure*
   a. Relationships between the sexes: age, other qualifications, ritual, form or type of unions, termination, and

stability of courtship, marriage, and alternatives to marriage; sexual ties as economic and social links.

b. Households: composition of domestic groups; sex and age roles and relationships; socialization patterns; interhousehold relations; permanence; developmental and age cycles.

c. Kinship: genealogical relationships; kindreds; kin ties and social networks; affinality; inheritance; succession; filiation; adoption.

d. Community: peer groups; voluntary associations; political organizations; leadership patterns; action-sets; religious groupings; social control; movements for social change.

e. Extracommunity institutions and relations: participation in government; political parties; police; courts; prisons; military services; labor unions; welfare system; health services; education; churches; mass media; social movements; gambling groups; friendship sets; other informal associations; ethnic intergroup relations.

5. *Knowledge, Belief, and Sentiment*

a. Socioeconomic values: aspirations; expectations; preferences; strategies for value maximization; ethical considerations; attitudes toward norm violation; authority orientations; political ideologies; orientation toward social change; attitudes on mobility and fluctuations of socioeconomic status.

b. Individual and group identity: content, quality, and tone of individual, role, community, social-class, racial, religious, and other identifications; concerns about strength, intelligence, autonomy, excitement, and routine.

c. Secular knowledge and world view: conceptions of extracommunity social worlds; knowledge and beliefs about history, the past, the future, luck and fate.

d. Health culture: conceptions and attitudes on health, illness, etiology, diagnosis, prognosis, therapy, body

parts and functions, psychological dimensions, public
and private services.
  e. Supernaturalism: beliefs and sentiments in relation to
    religious beings and forces, cosmology, mythology,
    ritual, magic, fate, ethical aspects, instrumental aspects.
6. *Communication and Socialization*
  a. Communication: linguistic patterns; art forms; institu-
    tionalized expressive behavior; other forms of emotion-
    al expression; mass media.
  b. Socialization process: infant care; child rearing; value
    inculcation; opportunities for role identification; indi-
    vidual life cycle.

SUGGESTIONS FOR FIELD TECHNIQUES

This is not the place for either a manual of ethnographic
techniques or an extended discussion of the relevant methodological literature. Nevertheless, it does seem in order to suggest a few techniques that may be appropriate for the particular kind of study envisioned here. Implicit in the repeated
earlier references to ethnography are a series of views on approaches to field work which should be made explicit. Much
of what follows reflects inclinations developed through the
ethnographic and other experience outlined in the Preface.
Thus no implication is intended that all ethnographers would
agree with these suggestions in their entirety. Indeed, there
would probably be lively debate on a number of points, some
of which will be indicated as we proceed.

Important among such arguable issues is the question of
optimum size and composition for a research team, not to
mention the question whether a team approach is necessary
at all. Outstanding work in urban slum studies has been done
by a single investigator working alone. On the other hand,
other well-qualified investigators have argued that coordi-
nated multiple participant-observers are required for successful field work in urban settings. The position adopted here is
that optimal results can be expected from a very small and
closely knit team. Such groupings might include married

couples, other pairs, or perhaps trios of ethnographers who know one another well and work together smoothly without serious organizational problems. The psychosocial problems of field relationships between researchers and subjects are quite sufficient so that further complications in the form of interpersonal difficulties among team members should certainly be avoided. To put it another way, in the kind of field work envisioned here, the ethnographer should be able to devote as much of his intellectual and emotional energy as possible to his relationships with the people under study. This in turn means that relations between fellow investigators should be of the positively stimulating and mutually supportive kind that obtain within a dyad or triad that has worked out most of its internal problems, rather than a complex team with unresolved status rivalries and other difficulties.

As already implied and as will be seen further below, the process of ethnographic study visualized here is a somewhat personal and individual one. This of course raises its own problems with respect to reliability of findings, observational and reportorial detachment, and involvement of the investigator in the social system under study. Ultimately the resolution of these problems depends upon the insight, maturity, and integrity of the ethnographers. If they report their methods carefully along with their data and interpretations, readers and users of their work can gauge these qualities and judge the value of the research accordingly. Working on these assumptions, ethnographers can expose themselves more directly and intensively to the cultural world they are studying than if they have to deal continually with an unwieldy team organization which tends to become a sort of intruding establishment interfering with relations between the researcher and his field of observation or inquiry. In other words, the team approach, especially when it is on a relatively large scale or incautiously organized, may well detract significantly from successful field work by creating barriers to essential research processes.

Many of the advantages which can be most convincingly

claimed for the large-scale team approach are essentially techniques for saving time, or increasing efficiency in the production of data, by adding personnel. Indeed, it is sometimes argued explicitly that a larger group of investigators is preferable because it can accomplish the same research task in less time than a smaller number, or an individual. The same principle less obviously underlies other considerations. Thus while it is true that two or more observers can view a system from more than one vantage point, it is also true that one skillful individual with more time can accomplish much the same object, though not with quite the same degree of simultaneity. Similarly, involvement with multiple factions or mutually exclusive networks can be accomplished either by fielding more personnel or by spending more time and exerting greater skill.

Moreover, spending longer periods in the field has its own independent value. It enables each individual ethnographer to observe more, carry out more extensive inquiries, absorb a greater variety of experiences, test and revise initial findings more fully, and comprehend better any changes that may be in process. The conclusion drawn here is that the approach through an individual or a well-tried small team not only compensates for drawbacks of the large team but also has important intrinsic value. This is certainly not to say that larger ethnographic teams have no useful functions. Clearly a large group is better adapted, for example, for obtaining simultaneously gathered quantitative information. It also seems clear that the choice is partly a personal one, in the sense that some individual personalities will function better in the one research context than in the other. Perhaps the main contention that could be widely agreed upon here is that efficient dyads or triads have their own unique value in ethnography that is probably not inferior to the utility of large teams.

An important key to procedures for obtaining the data needed is that the investigators should reside continuously in the area under study throughout the field research. This period of residence and research should not be less than one full year. The aim of these residence requirements is that the ethnographers should immerse themselves in the life of the people as directly, intensively, and continuously as possible. It is also intended that this experience should be of sufficient duration that the researchers come to know their subjects very well, have an opportunity to go through various stages of rapport and field relationships, and gain enough time perspective so that both seasonal cycles and at least any major trends of culture change become apparent.

While some highly qualified ethnographers would probably disagree on these next considerations, the experience mentioned above has left me with strong convictions about the role of the ethnographer. It is most advisable, I believe, that from the outset investigators should present themselves straightforwardly as anthropologists who have come to the area to learn as much as possible about its people and their way of life. Ethnographers should expect that they may have to explain what this means repeatedly, and that they may be asked many questions about their intentions and activities. Curiosity and sometimes suspicion, communicated perhaps as much by implication and indirection as by explicit query, will require self-presenting responses from the researchers. The principle behind such presentations and responses should be candor with respect to one's background, purposes, procedures, sponsorship, and related questions about the work. Through uninterrupted residence in the area, the ethnographers should work to see that their role becomes clear through experience of them as persons and of their activities as observed behavior, rather than through verbal explanations alone. Thus they may hope gradually to develop a place for themselves in the area as generally acceptable co-residents. This is likely to require an initial period of unpredictable length, during which time direct inquiries by the investigators should be kept to a minimum and directed only to topics they have no reason to believe are particularly sensitive.

It is suggested that the necessary positive rapport with the people of the area can be built gradually through contacts with neighbors, attendance at public events, and seeking out identifiable leaders. Casual contacts should be taken advantage of; informal and formal networks of association and communication should be followed wherever possible. When failures in building or maintaining rapport lead to frustration, the temptation to compensate by renewing ties outside the area must be strongly resisted. Resisting this temptation will help to insure that the ethnographer's needs for human association and companionship will reinforce rather than weaken his other motivations for building the necessary relationships with the community under study. While brief respites or vacations from field work may become necessary for various reasons, care should be taken that they do not interfere with the work any more than can be avoided. For social scientists who may be more dependent upon the conditions and associations of middle-class existence than they realize, these considerations may be very important. For these reasons, it is probably desirable that the research be carried out away from one's home city, that is, beyond easy reach in terms of ties with kinsmen, friends, colleagues, academic superiors, and employers. While these precautions have a certain aspect of artificiality about them, it may be only thus that the urban ethnographer working among the poor in his own society can approximate the absorption and immersion in the ethnographic process which comes about more easily, perhaps more naturally, in an exotic non-Western setting.

Every effort should be made to avoid entanglements that would lead to the channeling of early contacts with the people exclusively through one or a few individuals or institutions. The dangers of being unwittingly aligned or associated with particular factions or interests within the community will thus be minimized as far as possible. Among other considerations especially relevant to work with the lower-class poor, any association with the police, the welfare system, and other official agencies will probably have to be particularly avoided, as far as events allow. The main aim of these suggestions is to establish a realistic basis for the local people to regard the ethnographer as autonomous and trustworthy. It is taken for granted that the investigator will succeed more fully in this with some individuals and groups than with others. Moreover, relationships with one's subjects can be expected to fluctuate, both with time and as a result of events either within or outside the area under study. Indeed, in a sense the process of role establishment and rapport building can be expected to continue throughout the entire period in the field.

One of the earliest more or less technical requirements is to become as proficient as possible in the vernacular speech forms of the local people. The extent and difficulty of this task will obviously vary greatly from one research setting to another and in accordance with the background of the investigator. The first necessity here is to be able to talk to people in their own language and dialect, as well as to understand fully everything that is said within one's hearing. These considerations are as important for building optimum rapport as they are for the mechanics of information gathering. Depending upon the interests and training of the individual investigator, he might then go on to more systematic investigation and analysis of linguistic patterns. In view of all the academic and popular interest in the supposed verbal disabilities of the poor, and the many policy implications, particularly with respect to education, this could be a most important contribution of ethnography among the poor. This is particularly true because much of the contemporary controversy in this area is carried on without systematic knowledge of the relevant cultural context. Thus there is a great need for an approach to lower-class speech in which communication is treated as part of culture and linguistics as part of cultural anthropology.

In the general process of data collection, the principal procedures of inquiry should be a flexible blend of observation, interviewing, and participation. This combination of techniques can be continually varied to emphasize one approach or another as developing situations demand. It should probably be a conscious consideration of field method that regardless of varying emphases, all three components of technique will be in operation to some degree practically all the time. Thus whenever one is in contact with the people one should expect to be consciously observing their behavior. Similarly, in most situations one expects to engage in at least some minimum of verbal inquiry to help elucidate the immediate social situation, even when observation or participation is the dominant mode. Likewise, one strives to remain aware that all activities in the field may, to some degree, constitute participation in the life of the area, with possibly major effects upon what can be observed and what can be learned by asking questions.

Observation will be the dominant mode whenever direct perception and recording of individual or group behavior are practicable. This may be considered highly desirable with respect to every important social situation to which access can be gained. That is, a first principle of the ethnographic approach as applied here is that direct witnessing of ongoing social life is the preferable foundation of research whenever feasible. This requires establishing a relationship to the community such that one is admitted to and tolerated in the widest possible variety of social contexts, with a minimum of disturbing effect on behavior. This in turn depends upon lengthy acquaintance developed through exercise of skill in being unobtrusive and observant without attempting to conceal one's purposes. Much effort obviously must go into gaining access as an accepted observer to a substantial sample of households, to many peer groups, voluntary associations, and other institutional settings as well as the more public social events and group behaviors.

Interviewing as used here refers primarily to informal techniques of questioning and discussion. Mass survey procedures or precisely standardized schedules of questions are considered to be of secondary importance here. Most interview situations will be flexible and open-ended. In a sense nearly all contacts will be interview situations, for every effort will be made to use local participants and observers continually as informants, to provide verbal glosses and commentary with respect to ongoing behavior. The most extensive and intensive use of interviewing, however, will deal with matters either inherently or circumstantially beyond the range of observation. That is, there will be much questioning of informants to obtain biographical information, accounts of experience, data concerning modes of communication, and verbal expressions of beliefs, attitudes, and values.

Some interview procedures may be relatively standardized, such as collection of genealogical information or requests for household economic data. Many others will be entirely unstructured, developing as opportunities arise or situations occur in which minimally leading attempts can be made to elicit explanations of events, descriptions of how the world is conceptualized, and expressions of sentiments. Ethnographers expect that such informant work will assume a variety of forms that is quite unpredictable in advance. Hopefully there will be many private individual sessions, larger and smaller group discussions, some initiated by the investigators, others by informants, and so on.

By participation in the life of the research area, the ethnographer may hope to add a third dimension to his experience of existence in this setting. This is the element of personal involvement in the activities and concerns of the people under study. That is, he may come to know many of these people very well by sharing as much of their existence as they will allow. Here it is reasonable to anticipate informal visiting and neighboring between the investigator's own household and others, through which he may participate in some of the existing social networks. Each individual investigator should take advantage of opportunities to join in whatever group activities are possible by virtue of the researcher's sex, age, or other personal role characteristics. Wherever appropriate one should be ready to join voluntary associations. In situations where couples are normal units, as perhaps in some forms of evening recreation, husband-wife teams can participate jointly.

While none of these three approaches can be as sharply separated as they are conceived here, there is one element that belongs particularly to participation. As a participant one necessarily plays a role that has immediate results, and perhaps also long-range consequences, for the internal structure and workings of the group or network, including of course the interests of the other participants. This is clearly a problematical area of concern with much scope for variation in personal values and differences of opinion among field workers. As I see it, our aim in all participatory associations should be to play a role that is functional in the grouping or network as we understand it, that is as close to the normal roles of other participants as we find possible, and that at the same time minimizes our prominence or obtrusiveness in the ongoing social process as far as we can manage. By adopting these aims one can hope to gain some measure of direct subjective experience of life in the subsociety under study, while at the same time holding the distorting effects of one's presence to a minimum.

WIDER IMPLICATIONS OF FIELD WORK

This view of participation also makes it possible for the ethnographer, within the limits of his own value system, to act from the ethical position that he has major obligations to the people he is studying. He may feel these obligations simply in terms of an imperative to reciprocate the hospitality, time, effort, and forbearance which they have granted him in becoming his subjects. Or he may feel a closer identity with them as human beings or with their interests as he perceives them. These are among the senses in which the involvement of ethnography can mean an identification with the people whose life one attempts to study from within. It is in these ways that some ethnographers have become advocates or spokesmen for groups among whom they have worked, on occasion acting as vigorous partisans. There can be little doubt that such personal identification may deepen the quality of the ethnographic experience and lead to insights that would not otherwise occur. This certainly means that this kind of closeness to one's subjects can serve the intellectual aims of ethnography as well as fulfilling an ethical need. Yet it is equally clear that these involvements cannot be entered into lightly. They may easily become enemies of objectivity and a threat to intellectual balance or moderation. More important, the emotional, interpersonal, and practical consequences—for the ethnographer, for his work, and equally for his subjects—may be quite difficult to predict. Particularly in working with a subsociety as severely deprived, widely despised, and frequently opposed by conventional authority as the lower-class poor, the involved outsider must certainly be prepared for many situations of complex and difficult conflict.

Perhaps the most one can say here with some hope of broad agreement is that problems must be resolved by each fieldworker in terms of his own personality, individual values, and particular field experience. These issues are raised here, not from any ambition to resolve them with a universal formula, but rather because of an urgent sense that they should be given widespread attention, for too few students of poverty or culture are confronting these issues. These are among the problems that must be faced if we are to achieve an understanding of poverty and the poor that is intellectually sound and insightful, supportive of constructive and humane public attitudes, and conducive to humanitarian and progressive social policies.

Notes

These bibliographic notes are divided into two sections for each chapter. First, the numbered notes briefly identify the source of each passage quoted from other works. Second, unnumbered notes are used to identify additional sources either mentioned in the text or relevant as background material. The Bibliography (pp. 197–208) contains further details on all works cited in the Notes.

NOTES TO CHAPTER 1 (Pages 1–17)

1. Tylor 1871:1.   2. Goodenough 1963:259.
3. Warner and Lunt 1941:9, 14.   4. Honigmann 1963:191.

For a review of definitions of culture see Kroeber and Kluckhohn (1952). Cultural universals are discussed in C. Kluckhohn (1953). Several of Warner's works will be found under his name in the Bibliography; closely related sources are Davis (1946, 1952). One relevant discussion of values and world view is F. Kluckhohn (1950). The principal pioneer formulation of ethnographic field method is in Malinowski (1922; cf. Geertz 1967; Powdermaker 1967). Kroeber (1953) contains a number of review articles on field method. The phrase "culture of poverty" was coined by Oscar Lewis (1959 *et seq.*) and popularized by Harrington (1962). Among the many discussions of "lower class culture" are Gans (1962, 1965), W. B. Miller (1958), and Rainwater (1966*a–c*). Sources of related conceptions include Ireland (1966, "low-income life styles"), Keil (1966, "lower-class Negro culture"), Schwartz and Henderson (1964, "culture of unemployment"), Davis (1952, "slum culture"), and Bartky (1963, "dregs culture"). The cited interpretation of poverty and crime in our society is from Merton (1957). Among those who have criticized the conceptual confusion between culture and class are Hylan Lewis (1963, 1967), Ferman (1964), and Ferman *et al.* (1965). The variability of lower-class life and the doubtful value of focusing on motivational peculiarities of the poor are developed in several works by S. M. Miller and others (1963, 1964*a, b;* Miller and Rein 1965; Miller *et al.* 1965). Attention has been called to situational effects on value orientations by Rodman's notion of "value stretch" (Rodman

1963). Many of these issues are ably summarized and related to theoretical contexts in sociology by Rainwater (1966*b*) and Yancey (1965). Documentation of the contention that writing on the poor betrays middle-class biases will be found in Honigmann (1965*a*, *b*); Leacock (1967*a*, *b*); Rodman (1964, 1966); and Valentine (1966). Papers from the Anthropological Association symposium and related critiques of the poverty culture concept are expected to appear in a forthcoming volume (Leacock n.d.). Other recent critical discussions are considered in chapter 4 of this book.

NOTES TO CHAPTER 2 (Pages 18–47)

1. Glazer 1966:xi–xii.   2. *Ibid.*, p. xvi.   3. Frazier 1962:98.
4. Frazier 1966:367.   5. *Ibid.*, pp. 245, 255, 257, 259, 265, 267.
6. Glazer and Moynihan 1963:50.   7. *Ibid.*, pp. 63–64.
8. *Ibid.*, p. 84.   9. *Ibid.*, pp. 52, 53.   10. Moynihan 1965*a*:5.
11. *Ibid.*, p. i.   12. Moynihan 1965*b*:393.
13. Moynihan 1967*a*:36.   14. Moynihan 1965*a*:30, 47.
15. Moynihan 1967*a*:35.   16. *Ibid.*, p. 45.   17. Ellison 1967:12.
18. *Ibid.*, p. 18.   19. Moynihan 1967*b*:2.   20. *Ibid.*, p. 5.
21. *Ibid.*, p. 11.   22. *Ibid.*, p. 12.   23. *Ibid.*, p. 14.   24. *Ibid.*, p. 15.
25. W. Miller 1964 (quoted in Liebow 1967:227–28.)
26. Matza 1966:311.   27. *Ibid.*, p. 312.   28. *Ibid.*, p. 338.
29. *Ibid.*, p. 317.   30. *Ibid.*, p. 339.

Among the sources on the "Moynihan controversy," the Presidential speech referred to is in Goodwin and Moynihan (1965). Critical commentary on the Moynihan Report includes Carper (1966), Herzog (1966), H. Lewis (1965), Payton (1965), Riessman (1966), and Ryan (1965). The proposal for family payments will be found in the *New York Times* (1967). Estimates of the number of poor people in the nation are available in H. Miller (1964), Macdonald (1963), and Orshansky (1965), of which the latter is widely regarded as authoritative. Sources on children in poor families include U.S. Department of Commerce (1965) and Southern Regional Council (1966, 1967). Letters by Glazer and Moynihan replying to Ellison's critique appear in the August, 1966 issue of *Harper's*.

NOTES TO CHAPTER 3 (Pages 48–77)

1. O. Lewis 1959:15.   2. *Ibid.*, p. 16.
3. O. Lewis 1966*b*:xii. Passages from *La Vida* reprinted by permission of Random House, Inc. and Martin Secker and Warburg, Ltd. © 1965, 1966 by Oscar Lewis.
4. O. Lewis 1959:17.   5. O. Lewis 1966*b*:xxiv.   6. *Ibid.*, p. xxv.
7. *Ibid.*, p. xxv.   8. *Ibid.*, p. xxi.   9. *Ibid.*, p. xxvi.

10. *Ibid.*, pp. xxvii, xxviii.   11. *Ibid.*, p. xlvii.
12. *Ibid.*, pp. xxxii–xxxiii.   13. O. Lewis 1961: xxi.   14. *Ibid.*, p. xxi.
15. O. Lewis 1966*b*:xlv, xlvi.   16. *Ibid.*, p. xlvii.
17. *Ibid.*, p. xlviii.   18. *Ibid.*, p. 267.   19. O. Lewis 1965:434–35.
20. O. Lewis 1966*b*:xliii, li.   21. *Ibid.*, pp. xlv–xlvii.
22. *Ibid.*, pp. xxvii–xxix.   23. *Ibid.*, p. xlv.   24. *Ibid.*, p. xliii.
25. *Ibid.*, p. 1.   26. *Ibid.*, p. xlviii.   27. *Ibid.*, p. xlix.
28. *Ibid.*, p. 1.   29. *Ibid.*, pp. li, lii.   30. *Ibid.*, p. lii.

On the role of poverty culture concepts in justifying restricted educational opportunity see Fuchs (1966). For a theory of culture change through social movements consult Wallace (1956, 1961). In Lewis *et al.* (1967), which appeared after this book went to press, the reader will find an exchange between Lewis and sixteen other scholars on the merits of several works treated in this chapter. This exchange includes a spectrum of positive and negative reactions to the "culture of poverty" and related matters. Among the points mentioned by Lewis' critics are: the need for a clear distinction between class differences and cultural differences; the unanalyzed character of the massive biographical materials; the lack of specified procedures involved in eliciting the texts or of criteria for editing them; the doubt whether family-oriented biographical techniques are sufficient for discovering culture patterns; the question how representative the informants and their stories may be; the problem that the "culture of poverty" as portrayed by Lewis may be an ethnocentric middle-class stereotype; and the problem that this concept distracts attention from structural features of the whole society that severely limit the choices open to the poor. In reply Lewis offers no new data or fresh formulations. He does insist that his work must be understood as an indictment of the society, not of the poor. At the same time, however, he asserts categorically that the "culture of poverty" is also internally self-perpetuating. He also repeats his earlier assertion that it is easier to eliminate poverty than to do away with the "culture of poverty." Finally, he announces that during 1968 he will publish another book further analyzing "slum culture."

NOTES TO CHAPTER 4 (Pages 78–97)

1. Haryou 1964:313.   2. Clark 1965:xxv.   3. *Ibid.*, pp. 125 ff.
4. *Ibid.*, pp. 97 ff.   5. Keil 1966:5–6.   6. *Ibid.*, pp. 8, 10, 11, 12, 20.
7. *Ibid.*, p. 191.   8. *Ibid.*, p. 193.   9. *Ibid.*, p. 194.   10. *Ibid.*
11. Frazier 1966:367.   12. Gladwin 1961:75.
13. *Ibid.*, pp. 73, 74, 75.   14. *Ibid.*, pp. 76, 79.
15. *Ibid.*, p. 81.   16. *Ibid.*, p. 84.   17. *Ibid.*, p. 86.
18. Gladwin 1967:176.   19. *Ibid.*, p. 78.   20. *Ibid.*, pp. 95–96.
21. *Ibid.*, p. 26.   22. *Ibid.*, pp. 34–35.   23. *Ibid.*, pp. 168–69.

24. Liebow 1967:10.   25. *Ibid.*, p. 71.   26. *Ibid.*, pp. 135–36.
27. *Ibid.*, pp. 206–7.   28. *Ibid.*, p. 222.

NOTES TO CHAPTER 5 (Pages 98–140)

1. O. Lewis 1959:17.   2. Gluckman and Eggan 1966:xxvi.
3. McCulloch 1956:58.   4. Mitchell 1966:42–43.   5. *Ibid.*, p. 42.
6. Kroeber 1948:274.   7. Wagley and Harris 1955:442.
8. Steward 1967:24.   9. Gans 1962:243.   10. *Ibid.*, p. 244.
11. *Ibid.*, pp. 264–65.   12. *Ibid.*, pp. 268–69.   13. *Ibid.*, p. 268.
14. O. Lewis 1966*a*:19.   15. O. Lewis 1966*b*:lii.
16. Rainwater 1966*b*:40.   17. Keil 1966:10.
18. Ellison 1964:262–63, 271.   19. O. Lewis 1966*a*:19.
20. *Ibid.*, p. 21.   21. O. Lewis 1966*b*:xlvi.   22. *Ibid.*, p. xlvi.
23. *Ibid.*, p. xlvii.   24. *Ibid.*, pp. xlvii–xlviii.
25. W. Miller 1965:261–62.   26. *Ibid.*, p. 269.   27. *Ibid.*, p. 263.
28. *Ibid.*, p. 264.   29. *Ibid.*, p. 265.   30. *Ibid.*, p. 266.
31. *Ibid.*, p. 267.   32. *Ibid.*, pp. 268–69.   33. Goffman 1961.
34. Gans 1962:243.   35. *Ibid.*, p. 245.   36. *Ibid.*
37. *Ibid.*, p. 246.   38. *Ibid.*

General treatments of ethnographic methods will be found in
Malinowski (1922), O. Lewis (1953), Paul (1953), Powdermaker (1966),
Spencer (1954), and Williams (1967). Various techniques for studying
cultures "at a distance" are discussed and exemplified in Mead and
Métraux (1953). The anthropological literature prior to the 1960's on
relationships between larger and smaller sociocultural units includes
O. Lewis (1955), Marriott (1955), Ray (1959), and Redfield (1956). For
surveys of the more recent social anthropology of complex societies see
Eisenstadt (1961) and Banton (1966). Important older collections of
partial ethnographic studies in social anthropology include Forde and
Evans-Pritchard (1940) and Radcliffe-Brown and Forde (1950); more
recent examples dealing with complex societies are Bott (1957), Firth
(1956), Wolf (1966), Little (1957), Mayer (1966). The anthropological
focus on small-scale phenomena is emphasized by Evans-Pritchard
(1951), Firth (1951), and Benedict (1966). The concept of attenuated
affinality is set forth in Whitten (1967). Sources for some of the many
labels designating special "cultures" include Keil (1966, "Negro culture"), Davis (1952, "slum culture"), Snow (1963, "two cultures" of
science and other intellectual orientations), Irwin and Cressey (1964,
"thief" and "convict" subcultures), Bartky (1963, "dregs culture"), and
Bernard (1966, "externally adapted culture," "the unsocialized").
Recent general treatments and collections in the field of social stratification include Bendix and Lipset (1966), Ireland (1966), Kahl (1957),

Lipset and Bendix (1959), Merton (1957), Reissman (1960), Shostak and Gomberg (1964), Smelser and Lipset (1966), Warner (1953, 1957). By the recent eclectic literature on poverty I mean such works as Batchelder (1965), Elman (1966), Ferman *et al.* (1965), Gordon (1965), Harrington (1962), Hunter (1964), Kahn (1964), Lefcowitz (1965), H. Miller (1964, 1966), Riessman *et al.* (1964), Seligman (1965), Weisbrod (1965). Anthropological definitions and discussions of subcultures predating Kroeber's will be found in Linton (1936:272–78) and Herskovits (1948: 207–12, 574–77, 583–85). For preliminary reports of research on adaptations to poverty in a situation where ethnic variables are believed to be unimportant see Lex and Wolfe (1967) and Wolfe *et al.* (1967).

NOTES TO APPENDIX (Pages 173–89)

1. Mitchell 1966:41.   2. O. Lewis 1961:xv.
3. O. Lewis 1966*b*:xxiii.

Standard general outlines of cultural materials widely used by field-workers are Murdock (1959) and Royal Anthropological Institute (1951 *et seq.*). A recent introduction to field methods is Williams (1967). For discussion of the value of multiple participant observers see Lex and Wolfe (1967), Wolfe *et al.* (1967). For a viewpoint quite different from my own on the problem of self-presentation and the role of the field-worker see Berreman (1962). Additional sources on ethnographic method and technique are cited in the Notes for Chapters 1 and 5. Problems of subcultural linguistic distinctiveness are treated in Bernstein (1964*a*, *b*) and John (1966).

Bibliography

Arensberg, Conrad M.
  1955 American communities. *American Anthropologist* 57:1143–62.
Banton, Michael, ed.
  1966 *The social anthropology of complex societies.* New York: Praeger.
Bartky, John A.
  1963 *Social issues in public education.* Boston: Houghton Mifflin.
Batchelder, Alan
  1965 Poverty: The special case of the Negro. In Ferman *et al.* 1965. (Reprinted from *American Economic Review* 1965).
Becker, Howard S., ed.
  1964 *The other side: Perspectives on deviance.* New York: Macmillan.
Bendix, Reinhard, and Lipset, Seymour M., eds.
  1966 *Class, status, and power: A reader in social stratification,* 2d ed. New York: Free Press.
Benedict, Burton
  1966 Sociological characteristics of small territories and their implications for economic development. In Banton 1966.
Bernard, Jessie
  1966 *Marriage and family among Negroes.* Englewood Cliffs, N.J.: Prentice-Hall.
Bernstein, Basil
  1964a Social class, speech systems, and psycho-therapy. In Riessman *et al.* 1964. (Reprinted from *British Journal of Sociology* 1964.)
  1964b Elaborated and restricted codes: Their social origins and some consequences. In Gumperz and Hymes 1964.
Berreman, Gerald
  1962 *Behind many masks: Ethnography and impression management in a Himalayan village.* Society for Applied Anthropology, Monograph No. 4.

Bott, Elizabeth
   1957   *Family and social network.* London: Tavistock.
Carper, Laura
   1966   The Negro family and the Moynihan report. *Dissent,* March–
          April. (Reprinted in Rainwater and Yancey 1967.)
Castro, Janet
   1966   The untapped verbal fluency of Negro school children as ob-
          served through participant observation. Paper presented to
          the American Anthropological Association annual meeting.
          Forthcoming in Leacock n.d.
Clark, Kenneth B.
   1965   *Dark ghetto: Dilemmas of social power.* New York: Harper.
Davis, Allison
   1946   The motivation of the underprivileged worker. In Whyte 1946.
   1952   *Social class influences upon learning.* Cambridge: Harvard
          Univ. Press.
Eisenstadt, S. N.
   1961   Anthropological studies of complex societies. *Current An-
          thropology* 2:201–22.
Ellison, Ralph
   1964   *Shadow and act.* New York: Random House.
   1967   No apologies. *Harper's Magazine,* July 4:8–20.
Elman, Richard M.
   1966   *The poorhouse state: The American way of life on public
          assistance.* New York: Random House.
Evans-Pritchard, E. E.
   1951   *Social anthropology.* London: Cohen & West.
Fanon, Frantz
   1966   *The wretched of the earth.* New York: Grove Press.
Ferman, Louis A.
   1964   Sociological perspectives in unemployment research. In
          Shostak and Gomberg 1964.
Ferman, Louis A., et al., eds.
   1965   *Poverty in America.* Ann Arbor: Univ. of Michigan Press.
Firth, Raymond
   1951   *Elements of social organization.* London: Watts; New York:
          Philosophical Library.
   1956   *Two studies of kinship in London.* London: Athlone Press.
Forde, Daryl, ed.
   1956   *Social implications of industrialization and urbanization in
          Africa south of the Sahara.* Paris: UNESCO.
Fortes, Meyer, and Evans-Pritchard, E. E., eds.
   1940   *African political systems.* London: Oxford Univ. Press.

Frazier, E. Franklin
1932a The Negro family in Chicago. Chicago: Univ. of Chicago Press.
1932b The free Negro family. Nashville: Fisk Univ. Press.
1939 The Negro family in the United States. Chicago: Univ. of Chicago Press.
1957a Black bourgeoisie: The rise of a new middle class in the United States. Glencoe: Free Press.
1957b The Negro in the United States. Rev. ed. New York: Macmillan.
1962 Black bourgeoisie. 2d ed. with new Preface by the author. New York: Macmillan.
1966 The Negro family in the United States. Revised and abridged edition. Chicago: Univ. of Chicago Press.

Fuchs, Estelle
1966 The culture of poverty concept and education. Paper presented to the American Anthropological Association annual meeting. Forthcoming in Leacock n.d.

Gans, Herbert
1962 The urban villagers. New York: Macmillan.
1965 Subcultures and class. In Ferman et al. 1965.

Geertz, Clifford
1965 Under the mosquito net. New York Review of Books 9:4:12–13.

Gillin, John P.
1967 More complex cultures for anthropologists. American Anthropologist 69:301–5.

Ginsberg, Eli, ed.
1960 The nation's children. Vol. 1. New York: Columbia Univ. Press.

Gittler, J. B., ed.
1957 Review of sociology. New York: Wiley.

Gladwin, Thomas
1961 The anthropologist's view of poverty. The Social Welfare Forum, 1961. New York: Columbia Univ. Press.
1967 Poverty U.S.A. Boston: Little, Brown.

Glazer, Nathan
1966 Foreword. In Frazier 1966.

Glazer, Nathan, and Moynihan, D. P.
1963 Beyond the melting pot: The Negroes, Puerto Ricans, Jews, Italians, and Irish of New York City. Cambridge: M.I.T. Press and Harvard Univ. Press.

Gluckman, Max, and Eggan, Fred
1966 Introduction. In Banton 1966.

Goffman, Erving
  1961 *Asylums: Essays on the social situation of mental patients and other inmates.* Chicago: Aldine.
Goodenough, Ward Hunt
  1963 *Cooperation in change: An anthropological approach to community development.* New York: Russell Sage Foundation.
Goodwin, Richard N., and Moynihan, D. P.
  1965 To fulfill these rights: Remarks of President Johnson at Howard University. (Reprinted in Rainwater and Yancey 1967.)
Gordon, Margaret S., ed.
  1965 *Poverty in America.* San Francisco: Chandler.
Gumperz, John J., and Hymes, Del, eds.
  1964 The ethnography of communication. *American Anthropologist,* special publication 66:6:2.
Harrington, Michael
  1962 *The other America: Poverty in the United States.* New York: Macmillan.
HARYOU (Harlem Youth Opportunities Unlimited, Inc.)
  1964 *Youth in the ghetto: A study of the consequences of powerlessness and a blueprint for change.* New York: Harlem Youth Opportunities Unlimited, Inc.
Heath, Dwight B., and Adams, Richard N., eds.
  1965 *Contemporary cultures and societies of Latin America.* New York: Random House.
Herskovits, Melville J.
  1948 *Man and his works: The science of cultural anthropology.* New York: Knopf.
Herzog, Elizabeth
  1966 Is there a "breakdown" of the Negro family? *Social Work,* January, 1966. (Reprinted in Rainwater and Yancey 1967.)
Hoffer, Eric
  1964 The Negro is prejudiced against himself. *New York Times Magazine,* November 29, 1964.
Honigmann, John J.
  1963 *Understanding culture.* New York: Harper & Row.
  1965a The middle-class view of poverty culture, sociocultural disintegration, and mental health. Paper given at University of Kentucky Conference on Cross-cultural Psychiatry and Psychoethnology, Lexington.
  1965b Psychiatry and the culture of poverty. *Kansas Journal of Sociology* 1:162–65.

Horowitz, Irving L., ed.
1964   *The new sociology: Essays on social values and social theory in honor of C. Wright Mills.* New York: Oxford Univ. Press.
Hunter, David R.
1964   *The slums: Challenge and response.* Glencoe: Free Press.
Irelan, Lola M., ed.
1966   *Low-income life styles.* U.S. Department of Health, Education and Welfare. Washington: U.S. Government Printing Office.
Irwin, John, and Cressey, Donald R.
1964   Thieves, convicts, and the inmate culture. In Becker 1964.
John, Vera
1966   The Basil Bernstein fad. Paper presented to the American Anthropological Association annual meeting. Forthcoming in Leacock n.d.
Kahl, Joseph A.
1957   *The American class structure.* New York: Rinehart.
Kahn, Tom
1964   *The economics of inequality.* New York: League for Industrial Democracy.
Keil, Charles
1966   *Urban blues.* Chicago: Univ. of Chicago Press.
Kluckhohn, Clyde
1953   Universal categories of culture. In Kroeber 1953.
Kluckhohn, Florence R.
1950   Dominant and substitute profiles of cultural orientations: Their significance for the analysis of social stratification. *Social Forces* 28:376–93.
Kroeber, A. L.
1948   *Anthropology.* New York: Harcourt, Brace.
Kroeber, A. L., ed.
1953   *Anthropology today.* Chicago: Univ. of Chicago Press.
Kroeber, A. L., and Kluckhohn, Clyde
1952   Culture: A critical review of concepts and definitions. Papers of the Peabody Museum of Archaeology and Ethnology 47:1.
Leacock, Eleanor
1967   Distortions of working-class reality in American social science. *Science and Society* 31:1–21.
n.d.   *The culture of poverty: A critique.* Forthcoming.
Lefcowitz, Myron J.
1965   Poverty and Negro-white family structures. Unpublished manuscript.
Lewis, Hylan
1960   The changing Negro family. In Ginsberg 1960.

Lewis, Hylan—Continued
1963 Culture, class and the behavior of low income families. Unpublished paper presented to Conference on Lower Class Culture. New York.
1965 The family: Resources for change. Agenda paper No. 5, Planning Session, White House Conference "To Fulfill These Rights" November, 1965. (Reprinted in Rainwater and Yancey 1967.)
1967 Culture, class, and family life among low-income urban Negroes. In Ross and Hill 1967.

Lewis, Oscar
1951 *Life in a Mexican village: Tepoztlan restudied.* Urbana: Univ. of Illinois Press.
1953 Controls and experiments in field work. In Kroeber 1953.
1955 Peasant culture in India and Mexico: A comparative analysis. In Marriott 1955.
1959 *Five families: Mexican case studies in the culture of poverty.* New York: Basic Books.
1960 *Tepoztlan: Village in Mexico.* New York: Holt.
1961 *The children of Sanchez.* New York: Random House.
1964 *Pedro Martinez.* New York: Random House.
1965 Urbanization without breakdown: A case study. In Heath and Adams 1965 (Reprinted from *Scientific Monthly* 75:31–41, 1952).
1966a The culture of poverty. *Scientific American* 215:4:19–25.
1966b *La Vida: A Puerto Rican family in the culture of poverty—San Juan and New York.* New York: Random House.

Lewis, Oscar, et al.
1967 The children of Sanchez, Pedro Martinez, and La Vida: A CA book review. *Current Anthropology* 8:480–500.

Lex, Barbara W., and Wolfe, Alvin W.
1967 The effects of first contacts by researchers in urban field work. Paper presented before Central States Anthropological Society, 1967.

Liebow, Elliot
1967 *Tally's corner: A study of Negro streetcorner men.* Boston: Little, Brown.

Linton, Ralph
1936 *The study of man: An introduction.* New York: Appleton-Century.

Lipset, Seymour M., and Bendix, Reinhard
1959 *Social mobility in industrial society.* Berkeley and Los Angeles: Univ. of California Press.

Little, Kenneth
1957 The role of voluntary associations in West African urbanization. *American Anthropologist* 59:579-96.

McCulloch, M.
1956 Survey of recent and current field studies on the social effects of economic development in inter-tropical Africa. In Forde 1956.

Macdonald, Dwight
1963 Our invisible poor. *The New Yorker*, January 19, 1963. (Reprinted in adapted form in Ferman *et al.* 1965.)

McEntire, Davis
1960 *Residence and race.* Berkeley and Los Angeles: Univ. of California Press.

Malinowski, Bronislaw
1922 Argonauts of the western Pacific. London: Routledge.

Mangin, William
1967 Squatter settlements. *Scientific American* 217:4:21–29.

Marriott, McKim, ed.
1955 *Village India: Studies in the little community.* American Anthropological Association, Memoir 83.

Matza, David
1966 The disreputable poor. In Smelser and Lipset 1966. (Also in Bendix and Lipset 1966.)

Mayer, Adrian C.
1966 The significance of quasi-groups in the study of complex societies. In Banton 1966.

Mead, Margaret, and Métraux, Rhoda, eds.
1953 *The study of culture at a distance.* Chicago: Univ. of Chicago Press.

Merton, Robert K.
1957 *Social theory and social structure.* Glencoe: Free Press.

Miller, Herman P.
1964 *Rich man, poor man.* New York: Crowell.
1966 *Poverty American style.* Belmont, Calif.: Wadsworth.

Miller, S. M.
1963 Poverty and inequality in America: Implications for the social services. *Child Welfare*, November.
1964a The American lower classes. In Riessman *et al.* 1964. (Reprinted from *Social Research* 1964.)
1964b Some thoughts on reform. In Shostak and Gomberg 1964.
1964c Poverty, race, and politics. In Horowitz 1964.

Miller, S. M. and Rein, Martin
  1965   Poverty and social change. In Ferman *et al.* 1965. (Reprinted
          from *American Child* 1964.)
Miller, S. M., et al.
  1965   Poverty and self-indulgence: A critique of the non-deferred
          gratification pattern. In Ferman *et al.* 1965.
Miller, Walter B.
  1958   Lower class culture as a generating milieu of gang delinquency.
          Journal of Social Issues 14: 5–19. (Reprinted in Ferman *et al.*
          1965.)
  1964   Foreword. In Sydney E. Bernard, Fatherless families: Their
          economic and social adjustment. Brandeis University Papers
          in Social Welfare, No. 7.
Mitchell, J. Clyde
  1966   Theoretical orientations in African urban studies. In Banton
          1966.
Moynihan, Daniel P.
  1965a   *The Negro family: The case for national action.* Washington:
          U.S. Department of Labor.
  1965b   A family policy for the nation. *America*, the National Catho-
          lic Weekly Review, September 18, 1966. (Reprinted in Rain-
          water and Yancey 1967.)
  1966   Employment, income, and the ordeal of the Negro family. In
          Parsons and Clark 1966.
  1967a   The President and the Negro: The moment lost. *Commentary*
          43:31–45.
  1967b   The politics of stability. Speech to National Board, Ameri-
          cans for Democratic Action, September 23.
Murdock, George P.
  1950   Outline of cultural materials. New Haven: Human Relations
          Area Files.
New York Times
  1967   The case for a family allowance. *New York Times Magazine*,
          February 5, 1967.
Orshansky, Mollie
  1965   Counting the poor: Another look at the poverty profile.
          Social Security Bulletin, January, 1965. (Reprinted in Ferman
          et al. 1965.)
Parsons, Talcott, and Clark, Kenneth B., eds.
  1966   *The Negro American.* The Daedalus Library, Vol. 7. New
          York: Houghton Mifflin.

Paul, Benjamin
    1953   Interview techniques and field relationships. In Kroeber 1953.
Peyton, Benjamin F.
    1965   New trends in civil rights. *Christianity and Crisis.* (Reprinted in Rainwater and Yancey 1967).
Powdermaker, Hortense
    1966   *Stranger and friend: The way of an anthropologist.* New York: W. W. Norton.
    1967   Letter to the editor. *New York Review of Books* 9:8:36–37.
Radcliffe-Brown, A. R., and Forde, Daryl, eds.
    1950   *African systems of kinship and marriage.* London: Oxford Univ. Press.
Rainwater, Lee
    1966a Crucible of identity: The Negro lower class family. In Parsons and Clark 1966.
    1966b The problem of lower class culture. Pruitt-Igoe Occasional Paper 8, Washington University, Saint Louis.
    1966c Poverty and deprivation in the crisis of the American city. Pruitt-Igoe Occasional Paper 9, Washington University, Saint Louis.
Rainwater, Lee, and Yancey, William L.
    1967   *The Moynihan Report and the politics of controversy.* Cambridge: M.I.T. Press.
Ray, Verne F., ed.
    1959   *Intermediate societies, social mobility, and communication.* American Ethnological Society Proceedings, Seattle.
Redfield, Robert
    1953   Relations of anthropology to the social sciences and to the humanities. In Kroeber 1953.
    1956   *Peasant society and culture.* Chicago: Univ. of Chicago Press.
Reissman, Leonard
    1960   *Class in American society.* Glencoe: Free Press.
Riessman, Frank
    1966   In defense of the Negro family. *Dissent,* March–April. (Reprinted in Rainwater and Yancey 1967.)
Riessman, Frank; Cohen, Jerome; and Pearl, Arthur, eds.
    1964   *Mental health of the poor: New treatment approaches for low-income people.* New York: Free Press.
Rodman, Hyman
    1964   Middle-class misconceptions about lower-class families. In Shostak and Gomberg 1964. (Also reprinted in Rodman 1966.)
    1965   The lower-class value stretch. In Ferman *et al.* 1965. (Reprinted from *Social Forces* 1963.)

Rodman, Hyman, ed.
  1966 *Marriage, family, and society: A reader.* New York: Random House.
Ross, Arthur M., and Hill, Herbert, eds.
  1967 *Employment, race, and poverty.* New York: Harcourt, Brace & World.
Royal Anthropological Institute
  1951 *Notes and queries on anthropology.* London: British Association for the Advancement of Science.
Ryan, William
  1965 Savage discovery: The Moynihan Report. The *Nation,* November 22, 1965. (Reprinted in Rainwater and Yancey 1967.)
Sapir, Edward
  1924 Culture, genuine and spurious. *American Journal of Sociology* 29: 401–29.
Schwartz, Michael, and Henderson, George
  1964 The culture of unemployment: Some notes on Negro children. In Shostak and Gomberg 1964.
Seligman, Ben B., ed.
  1965 *Poverty as a public issue.* New York: Free Press.
Shostak, Arthur B., and Gomberg, William, eds.
  1964 *Blue-collar world: Studies of the American worker.* Englewood Cliffs, N.J.: Prentice-Hall.
Smelser, Neil J., and Lipset, Seymour M., eds.
  1966 *Social structure and mobility in economic development.* Chicago: Aldine.
Snow, C. P.
  1963 *The two cultures and the scientific revolution.* New York: Cambridge Univ. Press.
Southern Regional Council
  1966 Public assistance in the South. Atlanta: Southern Regional Council.
  1967 Hungry children. Atlanta: Southern Regional Council.
Spencer, Robert F., ed.
  1954 *Method and perspective in anthropology.* Minneapolis: Univ. of Minnesota Press.
Steward, Julian H.
  1965 Analysis of complex contemporary societies: Culture patterns of Puerto Rico. In Heath and Adams 1965.
Steward, Julian H., ed.
  1956 *The people of Puerto Rico: A study in social anthropology.* Urbana: Univ. of Illinois Press.

1967   *Contemporary change in traditional societies.* Vol. 1: *Introduction and African tribes.* Urbana: Univ. of Illinois Press.

Tylor, Edward B.
1871   *Primitive culture: Researches into the development of mythology, philosophy, religion, language, art, and custom.* 3d ed. 2 vols. London: Murray.

U.S. Department of Commerce, Bureau of the Census
1965   *Statistical abstract of the United States.* 85th ed. Washington: U.S. Government Printing Office.

Valentine, Charles A.
1964   Patterns of Negro residence, employment, and consumer behavior in Seattle. Mimeographed, Seattle Congress of Racial Equality.

1966   Anthropological study of the poor and ethnic minorities in the United States. Mimeographed.

n.d. (*a*)   Oscar Lewis' poverty culture reexamined. In Leacock n.d.

n.d. (*b*)   Alternative models for New World Negro cultures. In Whitten and Szwed n.d.

Vogt, Evon Z.
1955   American subcultural continua as exemplified by the Mormons and the Texans. *American Anthropologist* 57:1163–72.

Wagley, Charles, and Harris, Marvin
1955   A typology of Latin American subcultures. *American Anthropologist* 57:428–51. (Reprinted in Heath and Adams 1965.)

Wallace, Anthony F. C.
1956   Revitalization movements. *American Anthropologist* 58:264–81.

1961   *Culture and personality.* New York: Random House.

Warner, W. Lloyd
1953   *American life: Dream and reality.* Chicago: Univ. of Chicago Press.

1957   The study of social stratification. In Gittler 1957.

Warner, W. Lloyd, and Lunt, Paul S.
1941   *The social life of a modern community.* (Yankee City series, vol. 1.) New Haven: Yale Univ. Press.

1942   *The status system of a modern community.* (Yankee City series, vol. 2.) New Haven: Yale Univ. Press.

Warner, W. Lloyd, and Srole, Leo
1945   The social systems of American ethnic groups. (Yankee City series, vol. 3.) New Haven: Yale Univ. Press.

Weisbrod, Burton A., ed.
1965   *The economics of poverty: An American paradox.* Englewood Cliffs, N.J.: Prentice-Hall.

Whitten, Norman E.
  1967 Music and social relationships in the Pacific lowlands of
        Colombia and Ecuador. Paper presented at American An-
        thropological Association annual meeting 1966.

Whitten, Norman E., and Szwed, John, eds.
  n.d. Symposium on the New World Negro: Papers given at Ameri-
        can Anthropological Association meetings, 1967. Forthcoming.

Whyte, William Foote
  1943 *Street corner society: The social structure of an Italian slum.*
        Chicago: Univ. of Chicago Press.
  1946 *Industry and society.* New York: McGraw-Hill.

Williams, Thomas Rhys
  1967 *Field methods in the study of culture.* New York: Holt, Rine-
        hart and Winston.

Wolf, Eric R.
  1966 Kinship, friendship, and patron-client relations in complex
        societies. In Banton 1966.

Wolfe, Alvin W., et al.
  1967 Progress report on research into adaptations by urban white
        families to poverty. Mimeographed.

Yancey, William L.
  1965 The culture of poverty: Not so much parsimony. Unpublished
        paper, mimeographed.

Young, Michael, and Willmott, Peter
  1957 *Family and kinship in East London.* London: Routledge &
        Kegan Paul.

Index